God and Man at Work

God and Man at Work

Doing Well and Doing Good in the Bible's View of Life

Udo Middelmann

WIPF & STOCK · Eugene, Oregon

GOD AND MAN AT WORK
Doing Well and Doing Good in the Bible's View of Life

Copyright © 2013 Udo Middelmann. All rights reserved. Except for brief quotations in critical publications or reviews, no part of this book may be reproduced in any manner without prior written permission from the publisher. Write: Permissions, Wipf and Stock Publishers, 199 W. 8th Ave., Suite 3, Eugene, OR 97401.

Wipf & Stock
An Imprint of Wipf and Stock Publishers
199 W. 8th Ave., Suite 3
Eugene, OR 97401

www.wipfandstock.com

ISBN 13: 978-1-62032-935-1

Manufactured in the U.S.A.

Dedication:
With deep admiration I dedicate this book to my friends for almost half a century,

William Ted and Gladys Zane Smith

who set to work with God and shaped their life into a refined craft. With attention to detailed work and deliberate words they engage, encourage, and enrich many people and make merry many a heart. They open eyes, challenge minds, and welcome thoughtful talk: all in pursuit of greater fidelity to people, their world, and the God whose imagination and power created it, and whose passion is working to straighten it out again after Adam.

With strokes of paint, with flavors and textures of food, with lines shaped into letters for words and sentences between margins on the page, they lay out, each in their own way, a life of beauty and truth and welcome. They replace tiresome monotony with creativity, dusting off the furniture of the mind to give a shine to better ideas and color to a person's life. By their commitment and devotion to the real world they reduce the power and attraction of life's uglier corners.

Every person has a fundamental calling to be a human being, not less, not more. Most can pursue a genuine craft and, driven by their curiosity, lay the path that will support them from an idea to its realization. There is no magic or birthright to success, and neither life's circumstances nor people are always fair or just. But when all effort is committed to increasing knowledge and refining tastes, to study and memory, to the selection of distinct materials for diverse uses, we exhibit in practice that neither random selection nor fearful submission can give that honor, nurture, satisfaction and pleasure which each person craves and deserves.

Content

Preface | ix
Acknowledgments | xix

1 A Better Way of Seeing | 1
2 The Case for Moral Opposition | 11
3 Power Gained Through Knowledge | 18
4 You May Need to Check Your Glasses | 26
5 Someone There Before It All Began | 40
6 A Good Model for Governance | 52
7 Tragic Elements of Life | 64
8 Everyone a Craftsman | 81
9 Work and Effort Are Your Signature | 103
10 Laws Define and Restrain Evil | 111
11 Signposts for the Open Range | 122
12 A Lawful, Yet Untidy World | 132
13 Wisdom from Proverbs | 143
14 A House on Solid Rock | 151
15 A Distinct Ethical Edge | 165

Appendix
   1 *God and Man at Work* | 177
   2 *In the Beginning* | 182

Preface

ALMOST EVERY WEEK THE International Version of the New York Times publishes an interview with a person responsible for a business to tell what contributes to its success. Respect for people, accountability to high standards, honesty to clients, integrity of materials and admission of an occasional failure and steps taken to remedy it are frequently cited as of central importance for success and continuity. Giving people insight into the purpose of their work, additional training for advancement and fair wages express the care for people as human beings. They are human being and, unlike machines, not programmed means of production.

In this book I will lay out why an understanding of the practical and philosophical links between the world of ideas and professional efforts lead to greater success and rewards in the real world. Ideas always have consequences, but they bear fruit only when they shed light on and correspond to the shape of real things. Where people are respected in their skills and given explanations and the purpose of a task they will make a greater effort and render a better service. Success is neither genuine nor lasting when it is accomplished through deception and pretense. For personal pleasure, integrity and public reputation a product will only have lasting value and reward a person in human relationships when the substance of the service or product is true and corresponds to the desired quality and presentation. Eventually all deceptions will be laid bare, clients will go to other sources and satisfaction will disappear.

That is not always understood or encouraged. From snake oil vendors to promises of uncreated wealth so-called boosters portray an idea of fast profit and visions of power as real, only to find they are despised, feared and on the next occasion chased out of town. The desire for honest men and women requires a sufficient explanation to them of the wider context of life and the awareness of accountability to oneself from respect

Preface

to God, neighbors and the next generations. That context is best laid out in the Bible. Its text gives order to our lives from the confidence in the good creator of things and people, who addresses our minds with encouraging explanations which give value to the work of our hands in every effort to further a good and just life. The information appeals to our senses with a content that makes sense in light of the circumstances of our existence. It enlarges the field of our activities and brings together a view of the world in which we can be at home, do better and do good.

Every person wants to do well in his life and work. The first effort is always to succeed, to be able to manage around the cliffs and over the stones that are in our way. We want to stay above water and land on our feet. We seek security and ways to overcome hardships. We all strive to live, and even after disappointments we keep trying for some time. We want to figure things out and understand. We want to handle things rather than being intellectual and practical invalids by having our hands chopped off.

These metaphors from life illustrate our efforts to cope with and surmount difficulties on our way. Rocky cliffs and rough roads are in everyone's experience, but they do not set our horizon. Difficult surroundings encourage everyone to navigate with greater skill to more solid ground. Every person repeatedly looks for ways to overcome hardship, avoid danger and to make life somewhat easier in order to continue, to master and to enjoy it.

For in any arduous struggle in the face of real obstacles and needs every person sets out to develop coping skills. Adults will learn from instructions on how to recognize and address dangers, and with good ideas and gradually acquired behavior they will manage some things better. Adolescents will question what is done and copy or object to their human and natural environment. Even small children make every effort to crawl and stand, to speak and understand, to explore and discover and thereby to control their small world.

(Resignation and submission are responses that express later-in-life decisions to accept earlier failures and to make do, to conform, to abandon what is essentially human curiosity and to merge into One with a dominant power: the flow of history, the power and will of some deity, the traditions of the group, the belief in the superiority of one's community. Children are not by nature without inquisitiveness, questions and the deep need to understand).

While it is impossible to avoid all challenges and hardships it is not surprising that with the mind and manual skills people anywhere notice,

Preface

complain about and often oppose the various threats to life. Pain, tears and sorrow as well as better ideas start a process by which people reduce the dominance of what is unacceptable, though it may never be totally obliterated. Efforts for a healthy body and mind are part of essential human history everywhere.

While this is observable in general, we also notice that people somewhere cope better than in others situations. Some social and cultural contexts are less able, or perhaps willing, to discern what needs to be done in order to stand up to and master the variety of challenges to every life. At times the local setting, like the weather patterns or the lay of the land, the transport possibilities or isolation due to mountains or deserts, makes such efforts harder or easier. At other times, abilities or lack thereof, have their foundation in the world of specific and distinct ideas, in religions, in social patterns and intellectual assumptions.

While the former circumstances are of a more material kind the latter have more of an ideological/political or intellectual/spiritual cause. Material settings are more difficult to change, but can be substantially improved over time with much muscle, work and energy. Here we can think of the use of levers and wheels, draft animals, and physical/chemical improvements through clever engineering, daring trials and a will to overcome temporary defeat. It always amazes me to see that people built with giant rocks in Egypt, among the Hittites before 1200 BC or during the Minoan culture on the Peloponnese peninsula in Ancient Greece; or the clever ways to pump water out of coal mine shafts and to safely fly across oceans while eating lunch in the air. With similar drive we have learnt what chemicals to administer for the improved performance of the whole human body, including the brain.

Making different tools as extensions of our hands and feet is the way to go. We imagine them through clever ideas about the use of natural resources and then turn them into working objects. That same use of the mind, seeing through my mind's eye, also applies to efforts to reduce and overcome the kind of hindrances or impediments linked to thoughts and ideas, to beliefs and habits. They require an act of the mind and will. Needed is a shift in the world of ideas, the choice of a more fitting and wholesome moral/rational outlook about all aspects of human existence. For that we need to transcend the indications of the natural world with closed and regular patterns, and add ideas of what could or should be to the knowledge of what already is.

Preface

Material limitations affect all citizens in the same way. They are external to each person, part of the surrounding shape of things and observed with all our senses. By contrast, intellectual/moral/social limitations relate to individual choices and only then affect the person and everyone around them in the flow of history. They require thought, internal conversation and external debate for the consideration of alternatives or options in the way life is understood and pursued. The mind's eye can see and understand things differently. Alternatives are there considered, weighed and accepted or rejected.

Whether in the development of new means and tools or in the clarification of a more coherent and moral outlook, at the heart of the matter always lies a change of mind. At the origin of any notion that something needs to be done is a human being, a person who inhabits a world of thoughts and discerns between what is already, not yet or what ought to be instead.

The longing to do well, to find rewards for efforts includes a desire to make life less threatened and safer in a world where there is much failure, sorrow, pain and eventually even death as part of a less than hospitable natural world and, just as often, also from other people's neglect or cruelty. In addition there is the oppressive weight of view points and ideas that critique, bind a yoke on people and keep them tied up to traditions and beliefs with little encouragement to change the ways things have always been done.

What follows is an effort to understand the way all three sources of pain and frustrations wrap people into an oppressive net or cloth from which it is hard to untangle oneself.

What is needed is a way to discern and explain the abnormal elements in what seems so regular and normal in every human's experience, such as the frequent unfairness, the neglect by others, their quick judgment that everyone gets what he or she deserves; and then the violence of death against all life, the uneven personal skills and the surrounding painful limitations. Nature is what it is, but does not concern itself with care for people. All efforts to give nature a different shape come from people, not from nature itself.

People themselves do not live in natural harmony. They chose habits and make rules to introduce clarity and make engagement possible through language, schedules, work patterns and judges applying laws. Together each of these limitations reduces misunderstanding, rage, violence and someone's unchecked power determining what is right.

Preface

Each generation always teaches the next what they learnt, from daily survival skills to technical knowledge, and the framework for morals and meaning is passed on. Some people will invite and allow debate about the common or traditional ways, what they believe and how they understand the place of human beings in the order of things. Others will claim supremacy, power and position and use these to suppress any debate, discussion and contribution not already considered before. They will dictate what is to be repeated by everyone. Nothing new will be considered to address and reduce any of the three sources of hardship mentioned above. Such rulers, priests and parents are likely to operate from a closed mindset. Repetition is their insistence to maintain a predictable order: 'Do as I have done, say what I have told you to remember. Don't stand out of the collective, the clan, the culture and think for yourself. All people have always been in this situation, and you must not change it.'

By contrast I shall here help us to see an alternative, a possibility of real change through significant action and thinking imaginatively applied to real challenges. That gets done foremost by way of using our mind and emotion to picture something else, some other possibility, and thereby to question what seemed until now just normal, inevitable and necessary. The possibility exists, at the start of a life, to make choices in your mind to go another way, to change from the way of the past and to go in a more creative, enterprising and fulfilling direction. Here you are not a victim of circumstances, but at the origin of a direction that utilizes what you can learn, what you can dare to think and what you can carry out in a good measure to make tomorrow something other than a mere repetition of yesterday.

That view of human initiative and significance is born out in both human experience and Biblical confirmation. The teaching and the reality match up. Together they give two reasons for human creativity. This different view is quite unique to the Bible. In critical distinction to the program of the impersonal nature around us, or what most religions and secular ideologies teach as their main focus, the Bible tells people to play ball, to seek truth and justice for everyone. Only people in the image of the creator can take initiatives for change. Nature does not grieve, complain or shed a tear. Most religions and ideologies insist that you stick to the rules others have made before you, to not dance alone, to protect the community through obedience and repetition for the maintenance of known common practices. The Bible calls for human creativity, for a chosen honesty and for justice to God and Man in all things. There is

Preface

work to be done and rewards are to be celebrated. In a pain-riddled life here is good news, consisting of three insights:

Firstly, the Bible, the text that informs and shapes Judaism and Christianity, speaks of security through receiving God's calling: the knowledge that God created us to be individual human beings, called and mandated to discover, create and make useful what God has not already made himself: The God of the Bible is not oppressive power or imposing deity, but a creative, loving heavenly father, who delights in people and grieves when things go wrong, when people and nature suffer, and when a person is not given the respect he or she deserves as a thinking, feeling, and discerning creature.

In other words God did not create a static, repetitive and uniform universe, but a dynamic, changing world, in which he placed men and women together to live, think, create and love God and each other. That is the first good thing we learn in the Bible, and what a relief it is!

The second good thing is that God clearly tells us that things now are not what he had had in mind. Something went terribly wrong by the foolish, stupid and destructive choice Adam and Eve made, when they thought they also could be god. In other words, what seems now so normal to every one – real pain and hardships, death, contradictions, illness, bad leaders, lies and false pretenses – are not from God or have his approval. They are stones in our way and poison in our food. We must pray for wisdom and think what to do to remove them for ourselves and others. To attempt such efforts and to succeed is not against what God desires, but in line with his own work to reduce what causes so much suffering among people and within nature. People are meant to be agents of God's work and to resist any form of corruption, even death itself.

The third piece of the good news is that God addresses the problem and will solve the agony. Adam's and Eve's fault lead to guilt, which God removed through taking that guilt and paying for the consequences himself through the death of his Son. The material consequence of guilt still remains in the reality that death is everywhere in and around us. Everything is fractured, broken, damaged, and imperfect. The Bible holds out real hope that this will change powerfully when God will recreate the fullness of each person's life in a healed natural world. We already saw that power in real history when Jesus rose from the dead, talked with his disciples over lunch and appeared to more than 500 people off and on during 40 days prior to his ascension. As Jesus continued to live after his death and came back with a real body, so we are told is human life eternal.

Preface

We shall again live the way God had intended all along. There will again be people with real, then renewed, bodies to work, eat, make music and tools, and to love undisturbed and without what we now experience as constant frustrations.

Your life, your mind and your body, your choices and your manual, intellectual and artistic skills have a genuine calling and continuity. It is not ever all in vain!

How it all fits together and how we can know it to be true is what I want to lay out in this book. I will show that the Bible is the only real encouragement, on every level of what makes you a person, to develop your social capital. What is meant is that you change, increase, develop who you are as a person, an individual, a choice maker, among neighbors, when you use your head, your *caput* (Latin for 'head'), your reflections, ideas and concerns, in order to become more valuable to yourself and to the world around you: i.e. other people, to God the creator, in the care of creation and in the intellectual world of thoughts and ideas, of values, aesthetics and law.

You are familiar with terms like 'Social', 'Capital', and 'Development' and already have ideas about them. They are part of most people's vocabulary. They relate to our moral and political thought world and discussion. However they often bring to mind different ways of improving the way people organize themselves and engage the world around them. Whether put together as a phrase to formulate a concept, or in their separate notions, the terms grew on the fertile intellectual soil of Jewish and Christian thought with its affirmation of individual worth, the nobility of work and effort in a purposeful and linear history. In either form the terms suggest something of a progressive effort by either individuals or a society to step out of a mentality and experience of repetition into the pursuit of innovation and invention. When this way is engaged, reasons for complaints are met with resolutions. Through greater abilities confidence is gained.

An 'again and again' society, as Daniel Boorstin called it, has steady forms and a regular beat, but is also poorly motivated and equipped to seek changes for the better. It follows a "belief that history is governed by its own iron rules, and that man is not free to shape his own experience".[1] By contrast, social capital development expresses a desire and a mandate to improve the life in all areas for everyone. Starting with individuals and investing in their principle capital, i.e. their minds and skilled hands, in the end everyone will benefit from advances in health care, from education,

---

1. Daniel Boorstin, *The Seekers: The story of Man's continuing quest to understand his world*, pg 54.

business opportunities and social interaction under the rule of law, and free from the prison of unquestioned and unchallenged circumstances.

The teaching of the Bible is about God and Man, about a history to be created rather than to be suffered, about the need for the same law to protect everyone, and about the mandates to choose life rather than death[2]. That and more is the concern of the Bible's God. The text lays out a way to live rather than to always be a victim of circumstances, whether in nature or as a result of anti-human ideas and their consequences. Where it was read and embraced, it gradually transformed various peoples from their inherited views, whether Greek and Roman high-class paganism in Europe, or traditional tribal religions calling for passive conformity and with that justifying widespread suffering. Apart from Scripture the common refrain prescribes efforts to lose the individual person in a sea of a universal Oneness, a unity of all Being. This is the core teaching of Asian religions and the view of a necessary, scientific movement of 'dialectic history' in Marxism. Both of these surface already much earlier in ideas taught by Aristotle about 'nature in motion,' by Plato's outer-worldly 'ideal forms' or models, by Empedocles' view of four basic controlling elements of earth and air, water and fire. They were adopted in medieval concerns about the finite person merging with the Infinite in some future spiritual world. Buddhism and Marxism abandon the significance of the person in favor of an inevitable and impersonal final Unity of Being.

Jewish and Christian views, by contrast, are both more demanding and more respectful of each individual. God in that text is indeed mindful of people who are made lower than angels, but are above all impersonal nature.[3]

The Jewish and Christian Bible, though not always the whole church, confronted these dissatisfactory propositions and spoke of the nobility of each person, of the freedom and mandates to project life and justice into first an unfinished and then also an imperfect world. It drew its intelligence and hope from a unique and historical God, who empowers societies to gradually rise out of the passive experience of natural conditions and cultural enslavement. God calls people to purposeful and moral efforts. They were to create culture and set it into nature.

With that in mind, 'social' now expresses more than an existing community of language and customs found in every tribal society. Now it also

2. Deuteronomy 30:11–20 ; Luke 24 :5.
3. Psalm 8.

contains obligations to diminish the unfair experiences of life through law, love and the liberal practice of being "my brother's keeper"[4]. 'Capital' begins with human capital and is not limited to money and investments in machines, markets and products. Drawing on its original Latin meaning: the head ('caput'), the emphasis is on the mind, the thoughts and skills central to a person's significance, where we find tacit knowledge, a self-conscious awareness of possibilities, and a repertoire of procedures that are second nature to a person.

The notion of "development" can only be understood in the context of an un-repetitive, progressive and linear view of history. The Bible gave that to human culture, opposing both Greek views and secular or religious totalitarian traditionalism. Development is only possible where people are encouraged to participate with their creative minds in the market with innovations, and in democratic efforts to improve law and government for a more civil society.

Such open doors are central to the Jewish and Christian view of the world. Both communities are encouraged to argue with God, and everyone with each other and their historic situation. They compete for advances in quality and clarity from the perspective that every task remains unfinished. Without such efforts the development of social capital, the improvement of human conditions, will continue to stay behind or even fail.

Notice to customers found in a Manhattan store: "When you enter this shop take off your coat and roll up your sleeves. We work and like it. This shop aims to maintain the same atmosphere that is found in a commercial shop. There will be some noise as this is a busy shop, but there will never be disorder. Conversation in a quiet tone is permitted, but needless chatter is barred".

---

4. Genesis 4:9; Lev 19:16, Deut 21:1–9.

Acknowledgments

WITHOUT THE ENCOURAGEMENT AND support of Doug Kiesewetter, CEO of Brightleaf Technologies, Inc. this book may never have been written. We had met many years ago for one short, but intense conversation about the power of ideas to shape people's decisions, lives and attitudes. In subsequent years he had seen a growing need in his contacts with pastors, government functionaries and business leaders in the inner city and the developing world, who are long on devotional fervor, but short on holistic connections to the whole counsel of God.

Consequently this text sets out to gather the Bible's information about all of life into a manual somewhat like a curriculum to help such people bring a Biblical view to their efforts of improving life and work habits, building social capital and defining company cultures. The explanations from the Creator about reality will shape practical, intellectual and personal consequences for lasting benefits.

That "Ideas have Consequences"[1] is widely acknowledged. Ideas about life and death, work and time, authority and responsibility weave themselves into patterns of behavior, efforts and hopes. Ideas about power and law are reflected in what remains of Roman and Greek ruins. Some buildings on the tip of Manhattan still reveal Dutch insistence on their trading presence. More recent buildings of shipping companies and the Customs House tell of New York as a center for world trade. Gothic window frames on towering bank buildings speak of their competition with Trinity Church Wall Street next door. In Cologne, the vast steel and glass roof over the train station claims for human industry a similar admiration and wonder as was intended for God by the Gothic Cathedral next door.

Biblical ideas give information first to the mind, that most precious resource of human beings. Like letters from a distant friend, the Bible

---

1. *Ideas Have Consequences*, Richard M. Weaver, University of Chicago Press, 1948.

Acknowledgments

explains the larger context of a now damaged world, in which our lives play out according to things fixed and open. Our form as people, our gender and time of birth are part of a given inheritance. But the text also speaks and confirms our freedom and concurrent responsibility, to make us wise for prudent and effective choices that will shape part of the inheritance of the next generation.

Belief is not a membership in a religious association with club rules for comportment. From the start, the Bible calls people to live as human beings with solid, good and creative ideas in fulfillment of their purpose or calling, their design or nature, and with mandates to increase their abilities. Unlike everything in an impersonal nature human beings are choice-makers, able to reflect, conceptualize, weigh arguments, explore alternatives and discover with the great resource of a lively and trained mind new varieties and alternatives in lives of their creation.

I am very grateful for the skill and passion for language of my friends Lloyd and Libby Davies, who have explored my ideas for many years through study and in friendship with my family. Without their editorial work to improve the clarity of the text it would not be as fine a tool for its intended purpose.

I would be amiss if I failed to acknowledge also the many at home and abroad, who through their skill and determination crafted an inheritance for me and others in the human race. They remind me daily of the uniqueness of human beings, not proceeding from nature but made of dust with the life-giving breath of the God, whose image every creative person bears. I thank foremost my wife Deborah and my family who, each in their unique and reflected way, break the predictable pattern of repetitions with thoughtful efforts to press their ideas into skillful shapes to mark our common history; and everyone who like the man in a side street in Hyderabad could fashion for my locked suitcase within minutes, with only a copper wire and a hammer, a replacement key for the one a beautiful little beggar girl had stolen from my pocket, while distracting me with gorgeous cartwheels for a few coins . . . which I had just given her out of the same pocket.

Udo Middelmann
January 2013, Gryon and New York

Chapter 1

A Better Way of Seeing

EACH PERSON, WHETHER ALONE or in a community or culture, establishes specific ways to see and relate to the world around them. Patterns that determine action across the full spectrum of life are formed by how a person describes and responds to the world. Most people seek to do well and establish patterns that help them succeed, including ways to diminish some of the pain and insecurity everyone experiences as part of being alive. We all develop daily habits, make schedules, and use words in our language, learning to think and work with increasing skill.

Such responses to other people and things, to time and work, to life and death are very rarely natural or instinctual in human beings. They often vary greatly from place to place, and person to person. They are in fact chosen, born out of our interaction with what we perceive can make life easier and then passed on from one generation to another in words, rituals, and laws. At times they can be changed, improved, or neglected.

These patterns of speech, work, and belief exhibit a wealth of ideas about the real world which, whether true or false, become familiar and are then followed throughout life. They are ways of seeing and doing adopted to help understand and master a rough, insecure world. Because of the fear of insecurity that comes with any innovation, methods of coping are often repeated from one generation to the next and barely changed. But when people resist the fear, seeking ways to diminish it, they frequently become safer, less exposed to the rough, dark valleys common to our human experience.

There are of course also external influences such as weather, geography, transportation, and exposure to a wider circle of people through trade, literature, and intermarriage. Yet the human mind is most central in shaping the habits and attitudes of people. The unique inner life of the self, the mind as well as the heart of each individual, is crucial to the network of powerful ideas which give direction to life and work, to love and responsibility, to thought and training.

Whether we submit as victims or rise to master our own lives depends on how we understand reality and determines our place in the scheme of things over time, either depressing or encouraging us. When we accept the calling to stand out as creative and morally significant, our world will gradually and significantly change, and become more habitable. However, where natural forces dominate, moral concerns always play a smaller role. Physical and political power tends to oppress or even crush the weaker links in society, who are forced by religious and social domination to accept their situation. They find no fulfillment and few rewards; they leave only traces of human presence on the windy surface of history, and their bones in the ground.

A More Respectful Point of View

There is a distinct outlook which over time laid a much more solid foundation for our existence and created the legal, material, and intellectual support necessary for a high view of the individual as a person with a unique calling to think, work, and take responsibility for history shaped by human action. A specific composite of unique ideas about human rights, human worth, culture, and philosophy became pillars of wisdom and knowledge, bringing great benefits to people and their environment through the development of persons and their inhabited world. Together they have made the talk about human beings, human rights, human worth, and human culture and philosophy cohere. Even though change was imperfect, an increasing awareness of the effort needed to improve the human condition across all areas of life gradually occurred.

Where these ideas were brought together, intertwined like a rope of many strands, they enabled people to assert themselves, introducing greater cultural, and economic, and social responsibility. For that to happen people had to free and assert themselves. They needed the benefits that follow from greater freedom, from natural bondage, from fate or divine control, from geographical circumstances, and the watchful eyes of previous generations, and from the philosophical dictates of an arrogant ruling class. In Medieval Europe, during the eleventh and twelfth centuries, the controversy over investiture privileges between the two powers of Pope and Emperor, both often decadent and unreliable, benefited from independent minded noblemen, traders, craftsmen, and bankers as well as the growth of markets, universities, and expanding cities. Central authority was weakened as competition gave rise to greater energy, invention, and new ways of earning a living.

The rediscovery during the Renaissance of older sources of philosophic reflection and insight, and the Reformation's return to a vibrant Christianity of intellectual honesty rather than religious formalism, led to doubt about assumptions and a longing for something more true to the real world. Expanding trade and engagement with a wider world added to people gradually awakening to the rightful use of their minds, their will, and their hands to improve life, to leave the rut of repetition and submission, and plough new fields with greater possibilities. The discovery of new continents and peoples, new means of travel and trade, new tools and the benefits of education in the first universities, all supported a dynamic sense of enterprise that gave the whole of Europe new horizons.

No longer entirely based on a controlling formula, life became an experiment in the pursuit of untidy creativity. The tidy restrictions of hierarchical authority structures, which were often immoral and dishonest, gave way to a system of laws to which everyone was now accountable. The weak laborer became stronger through the application of common law as even those in power had to comply.

Under the teaching of a more accessible Christianity, new political and intellectual circumstances gave significance to individuals, and both fatalism and resignation were questioned and increasingly refuted. A desire for greater control over sickness and health also grew as the protection of the body through hygiene and a more varied diet became part of a more decisive care for life. The Enlightenment itself resulted from the light of reason, research, and newly understood religion, an understanding largely due to the Protestant Reformation and its central respect for the human being. The rediscovery of the Biblical call for people to be real human beings, and to accomplish the good and the just as God's agents replaced what had been lacking in earlier systems of thought which had demeaned, insulted, and oppressed people through fear: fear of life and death, of others, of gods, and of God.

From Word to Work

A new work ethic resulted from a word ethic, which was proclaimed in sermons not only on religious subjects, morality, and fear of punishment, but also on our real-life obligations to exhibit skillful craftsmanship from respect for God's deliberate and specific creation, and for the benefit of our neighbor's life. The understanding grew that reality is complex, that we are to be at all times responsible and creative persons.

The teaching of historic Biblical Christianity explains the origin and purposes of humanity. It confirms the reality that God's creation functions in a way that can be scientifically known. It also reveals that we should love our neighbors as ourselves, and respect everyone's right to their own calling. The Bible lays out the causes and calamities of life in a fallen and therefore damaged world which God has not abandoned to itself. We find in this text a factual basis for hope in God's continuing work to reclaim, redeem, and eventually also repair His creation.

In the following chapters we will consider further this astonishing interplay between the clearer views of reality achieved through study, work, and enterprise, and the singular contribution Christianity has made toward that pursuit. Far more than a mere manual of the heart to find personal peace, the Jewish and Christian Scripture is first a book of propositions, of information. By laying out an intellectually coherent view of the reality we all know, the Bible has shaped the outlook on persons and their activities for many societies to great benefit. It presumes that intelligent people will seek to do good and resist evil because they can be confident of God's real existence and favor, expressed in his calling to us to be human beings.

Such confidence grows gradually. From early childhood we learn, through our parents and others, and by our own curiosity, how the world around us functions; this project occupies us every day. We raise questions and receive information, discovering and collecting impressions, in order to gain skills and confidence. Only we human beings want to know more than the limited personal experiences of one lifetime. We also want to know the past and what might lie ahead. We wonder, in the sense of having many questions, but also in the sense of being amazed at what we can understand and accomplish.

Wherever we live, the world presents itself to us in many forms and patterns; it comes in different materials, alive and still, and includes each of us as human persons. As distinct human beings we share this world first with neighbors like us, and then with animals and inanimate things both small and large. Unlike impersonal things which largely remain the same over time, or animals which behave and change in accordance with their natures, we humans have few instincts to help us cope and to direct our behavior and actions into the external world. We are not born with automatic insight, but must learn how to reach the goal we first had in our mind, of safe and meaningful lives: to breathe and eat, to be secure and healthy, to think wisely and relate to others with loving trust. Because our way of life must be learned, we depend on information and instructions to help us find direction and make sense of existence.

On Being and Becoming Human[1]

The process of becoming a human being is a complement to our biological birth. Our brains need to develop in a specific manner and direction. They need to become thinking and discerning minds in order to be able to evaluate, imagine, and make distinctions responsibly. We slowly learn concepts and words to orient us in the world. Human beings, you and I, need sufficient comprehension of facts plus the motivation to will what is right, good, and just, all of which we must acquire through critical thinking, careful observation, and the tools given to us by a real education. These will liberate us from being slaves to nature and the unquestioned traditions, superstitions, and fatalistic worldviews of many religions. Socrates thought the unexamined life is not worth living[2], and Jesus Christ argued with many Pharisees because of their frequently unexamined and therefore often illogical pronouncements.[3]

Once we understand things as they are we must also determine to accomplish good and abstain from bad actions in an ongoing history. That determination must come from seeing that life is a calling and has fundamental value, and meaning; it is not merely an accidental occurrence in a meaningless flow of history or biology. We cannot watch like idle observers while good and bad people, or better and worse natural settings press on us. Time and circumstances do not stand still: we must cease being victims and take charge of our lives.

---

1. The subtitle of Willard Gaylin's excellent book *Adam and Eve and Pinocchio* (Viking, 1990).
2. In Plato's dialogue, "Apology," fifth century BC.
3. e.g. Matt 12:3ff and 12:22ff.

In each period of history and on every continent the intellectual freedom to respond to life as an individual calling is singularly found in societies where a biblical perspective on life, work and community shapes people's thoughts and actions. This view propagates a high value for each person, male and female, young and old, strong and weak. It is the foundation for law, economics, and education, for respect and compassion, and for the advancement of human life in a burdensome world.

This view stands in contrast to the many fatalistic attitudes among those influenced by other cultural and religious outlooks which lead to a closed, deterministic, collective mindset and present a unified master plan of unquestioned rules and patterns that stifle initiative, preserving bad habits, and leaving little room for the exceptional individual. Such closed-system perspectives are typical of religions around the world, whether they deal with spirits and invisible forces or with matter and energy as the final stuff of reality. They all link the person to a larger whole or a unity of Being (in the sense of "whatever is") whether that is a god, the whole universe, unchangeable tradition, or scientifically observed interactions of mere matter.

The Biblical view is that a person is more than the sum of his parts: life transcends physics and chemistry.[4] We need the initial tools of logic and sequential thought, of precise observation, imagination and reflection in order to function and make decisions through the exercise of the will. If we are to become wise, good, and responsible, the brain we are born with must be developed through stimulating arguments and detailed explanations, long conversations, and sensible ideas expressed in full grammatical sentences that accompany every effort of practical love. Only then can the mind use the brain to direct the hands in all areas of life and work.

This is not always properly understood. When young children hear only a few repeated words and stories, they are exposed to narrow patterns of life and strict guidelines, but their need to understand things, to enter into conversation with all reality, is neglected from lack of enough defining words and distinct concepts. This approach promotes obedient submission rather than providing the stimuli and provocations that may lead to imagining alternatives. These children will become adults largely unequipped to act in creative, moral ways.

---

4. See Michael Polanyi's "*Life Transcending Physics and Chemistry*" (*Chemical and Engineering News* 45, August 1967: 54–66).

Obedience maintains established patterns of repetition and tradition but stifles critical thinking, enterprise and responsibility. Without these we are victims of circumstance, easily exploited by others, and often discouraged further by subsequent failures.

Complaining alone will not really change anything, nor lead to anyone being challenged or feeling guilty about another's condition. What is merely frequent will remain accepted as normal unless a more critical mind discovers good reasons for an alternative, and then finds the courage to pursue it.

Until quite recently many societies around the world bound the individual to hierarchical rulers and traditional life patterns shaped by various religious or materialist views. They required people to lie low in silence, to repeat only what had always been said, to live with what was visible on the surface or what they gathered from nature, with little encouragement to go further than what met the eye. Such people, while offered safety in a common belief, were locked into a cruel destiny with no possibility of escape.

Liberating Jewish Thought

Under the teaching of the Bible, cultures which for centuries had been closed experienced an astonishing spread of liberating ideas and habits. People began to look at life and history differently. This expanding view of a world enlightened by Jewish thought and Christianity, applied to all areas of life, work, and government, brought an awareness of possible abnormalities and wrongs, and opened the door to change. The Bible freed people from the prison of a determined, locked-in view, whether Greek philosophic thought, Marx's deterministic ideology of an inevitable material or scientific history, or religion. The Bible's view of God, man and history is different; according to the Bible, intellectual, cultural, and even political responsibilities are part of the calling of all men, women, and children. It locates the core of historic events, economic growth, scientific improvements, and moral political efforts in the heart, mind, and soul. Citizens, neighbors, parents, and children are respected as significant agents by God the Creator and ought to be treated thus by each other.

Here lies the foundation for all human individuality, fostered and preserved in the right to life, education, and justice by virtue of our existence, not granted by a state or international convention. The rule of law, respect for contracts, commitment to social responsibility, the freedom that comes from owning private property, and a partnership in government and family all reflect the high view that we are made in the image of the God of the Bible.

There are many good reasons to suggest that human beings are called to rise above the low and demeaning place forced on them by many cultures. Respect for ideas and work, and distinguishing moral from immoral choices are the singular fruits of biblical insight. Such a high view is related to the way the God of the Bible addresses us with content accessible through our minds. Words, accounts, and explanations communicate real meaning, giving reason a proper and valued place. Otherwise it is impossible to know how to live above "the push and shove" of circumstances and be freed from collective habits.

The information in the Bible is not primarily religious in nature; rather, it serves factual and historic purposes, and answers the basic dilemmas of life. It must be approached with a critical mind and the normal questions arising out of life itself: What is the nature of reality? What is the foundation for moral and cultural behavior? What can be claimed about the mind, rationality, and truth, life and death?

The Bible's Panorama

All manner of insights flowed from bringing these questions face to face with the Biblical perspective about common human reality. They led to responses of wonder, love, and fidelity, but primarily laid the foundation for a more humane, economically viable, and enterprising attitude in all domains of human existence. Just as the nutrients at the root of a tree determine its fruit, so the Bible produced as its fruit respectful, compassionate, imaginative, and enterprising people. Conversely, the absence of its instruction resulted in the withered fruit of people enslaved to their fate, their rulers, their natural conditions, and their repetitious practices.

A lively, active mind creates a mental distance from the impersonal, amoral world of things and animals, of the processes of physics and chemistry around us. From that distance we readily understand that thinking people are unlike anything else on earth. Only with our material bodies are we like the rest of nature, like sentient animals, organic plants, and physical rocks. Our unique strength lies not in our joints, bones, and muscles, but in our ability to think, to question, to doubt, and to

A Better Way of Seeing

imagine. Our minds are not limited to the present moment; we consider the past and the future as well, transcending the immediate instinctual response to what is in front of us by demanding reasons and anticipating consequences.

Given our distinct difference from animals, plants, stones, or the clouds above, we should not model our behavior on them but seek with our minds to understand and then weigh alternative actions. We will quickly see that we are not part of a collective, communal mind, but that each person has unique sensitivities, insights, questions, and abilities. We can free ourselves, at least in our thoughts, from our natural setting, from communal bondage, and from a culture of monotonous repetitive uniformity. While new ideas or choices may break the harmony of the collective, the village, or the tribe, it is only through the courage of individuals who explore more reasonable, beneficial alternatives that perceptible change and real improvements will occur. "If not you, then who? If not this, then what? If not now, then when?" are challenging questions, inherited from the Jewish worldview[5] to be considered by each liberated person. For it is always our questions that first crack open the seeming normality of painful, unfair, and unacceptable conditions. Only when sickness is recognized as a problem are explanations and remedies sought out.

Human minds respond with decisions born in the will. With strenuous effort we force ourselves to do what is right, to work, and even to choose to love. By an act of the will we attempt also to practice self restraint, patience, and coping skills to control our temper as if it were an unruly dog. There is a double-directional sovereignty in the human being; the power to will is not inherited, but must be chosen and carefully tuned up by exercising it just as we do our muscles.

Do we stand up courageously in our time against what impersonal nature around us seems to insist on, or not? What effort is justified to improve the quality and length of life? How do we address floods, drought, and sickness, or the provision of only monotonous foods? They are all natural, come from nature, but do not help us live well, or enough? How are we to understand the many frustrations in our daily lives? And what can we learn about limiting pain, conflict, and unfairness? How have people coped with hardship and death without always being victims who have lost all courage to consider a better alternative? Why have so many

---

5. A paraphrase of the famous saying of Hillel the Elder, first century B.C.

people chosen to join in pain a (dis)comfortable resignation which leads to continuous suffering, pervasive poverty, and early death?

These are questions of *economics:* the wider meaning of the word is composed of two originally Greek roots: household (*Oikos*) and law (*Noumen*). The household we are interested in is our life and everything that helps make it livable; law refers to the principles which give shape and direction to that life.

The next section explores how alternate economic worldviews affect attitudes towards life, work, and daily purpose.

Chapter 2

The Case for Moral Opposition

FROM AN EARLY AGE every person raises questions and pursues answers about how to understand and shape their lives. Everyone, including ourselves, constructs a basic grid that directs their economics in the wider sense in which I used the term above. This grid expresses our worldview and directs life's patterns, becoming a kind of ideology, whether secular or religious. We find answers and learn ways to see the world through the instruction and example of parents, teachers and accomplished professional masters, each of whom is enjoined to improve the skills of their charges. Teaching and learning are a part of being human. We imitate others to benefit from what each older generation has figured out. Certainly while still young, we do many things because we simply watch and admire them.

Such ways of adjusting to the social and cultural environment are evident everywhere. As children follow the example of their parents, so too we all link up with something bigger than ourselves by following the example and instruction of others. By participating in a language, an ethical and religious community, and a marketplace people hope to avoid or resolve the painful contradictions of existence. Communities of ideas and beliefs differ considerably in detail but all propose answers to the conflicts of life in the embrace of a collective understanding and learned coping skills.

Our senses perceive and recoil from the reality of pain. The Bible validates our complaints and objections, encouraging us to change the particular situation in the outside world that causes the pain in the first place. But some religions and worldviews suggest and actually teach that pain and conflict exist only in the mind and originate with the viewer;

they deny that there are real problems in the external world, which is either willed by a god or simply part of a steady pattern like the stars in the heavens and the tides in the sea. Such beliefs, taught by most religions and secular materialist worldviews, hold that "everything is both necessary and inevitable, and part of a normal, regular pattern ordained by the gods, nature, or history. For people who believe in a divinity, events in history may be seen as punishment for earlier failures. For others, whatever happens is just part of a sequence of natural events or of a larger process of dialectical history. In every case, each person's experience is determined by fate, whether through the working of some malevolent force or a simple selective process in an impersonal nature.

It is thus always our perspective which must change in order to submit to and accept whatever happens. The switch from objection to denial must occur in the mind, in one's consciousness.

Submission to the inevitable is required, and personal experience and complaint are effectively nullified in sacrifice to a larger cause. With a change of mind and belief everything becomes acceptable.

Suffering in Silence Or in Public

In contrast to Christianity and Judaism these beliefs logically demand an enforced indifference, a blind acceptance, a powerless resignation. Life's pain is all in our heads, in our way of seeing things, not in the way things really are; everything has its unavoidable place or course, all is normal in the larger scheme of things. The only solution is learning to ignore pain, abandoning rationality and criteria of justice, and accepting that everything as originally intended or deserved is equally good. Nothing is ever truly wrong with an individual's experiences; therefore, all forms of resistance are self-inflicted and unnecessary.

These widespread views squash any active search for ways to reduce suffering in the external, real world. In contrast the Bible presents a genuine and more workable alternative. It offers a very different way of understanding life that elevates the person to become an agent of review, revolt, change and renewal. It affirms that injustice, unfairness and damage in all of life are not mental illusions. Between birth at the start and death at the end, life truly is difficult, unfair, painful and often futile. Both our life

The Case for Moral Opposition

experience and the Bible acknowledge reality for what it undeniably is[1]. The distinctions we make in our minds and express in words and actions correspond to real distinctions which we all encounter in the real world.

We are then encouraged to actually affect that damaged reality by making moral decisions and using realistic and fact-based options. A change of heart and creative efforts can overcome real problems and bring greater benefits and satisfaction than denial or unquestioning acceptance. The Bible liberates us from resignation to every status quo and the unjustified authority claimed by a false god, man, or nature.

Like a stage description for a play that introduces the scene and the characters, the Bible lays out at the beginning the contrast between God's original plan for creation and what went so terribly wrong afterwards.[2] It enables us to see that the present state of the world is not what God intended, nor has it always been this way. What we know and experience today should not remain unchallenged. The distinction between "before" and "after" makes any one event less typical, absolute, authoritative or final. Consequently, we can see reality with a sharper, more distinct focus. Not everything is part of a universal One, the will of a god, part of a natural and unstoppable material evolution or Providence. With reality subject to review, the door is open to a very different proposition about how to live and work without always being crushed by an absurd, unfair, meaningless situation which seems permanent and irresolvable.

The Nature of Truth

The idea that the Bible is the root source for practical life is at odds with the common presupposition that it is only a religious book. Yet, starting with Genesis nothing in the Bible demands to be religiously believed. Its supporting evidence comes from what is closest to us, our own objective reality. It consists of the interlocking evidences of our individual consciousness and the experience of the shape and functioning of the external world, regardless of what anyone thinks of it. Francis Schaeffer called these unavoidable factors "the Universe and its form, and the mannishness of Man."

---

1. Thomas Hobbes (1588—1679), in *Leviathan* (1651): "and the life of man, solitary, poor, nasty, brutish, and short."
2. Follow the rapid deterioration of reality from Genesis chapter one to chapter four.

Belief in the truth of the Bible does not make anything more true, just as believing the earth is flat does not make it so. The Bible's propositions are either true or false. It acknowledges reality as it already exists, not as make believe, and then goes on to show that God is not a liar. It explains the painful contradictions in life and urges us to fight to overcome them, not through religious faith or repetitive ideological affirmations but through moral, intellectual and practical action.

The Apostle Paul prays that believers would increase in understanding,[3] not in their ability to pretend that things are not as they are. He encourages us to change things rather than to go the easy route of ritualistic repetition from ignorance of alternatives. Moses, Jesus and Paul teach a different way to think, see and live, based not on religious belief but on better comprehension of the place human beings have in the real world. These teachings draw strength from their witness to the reality created and observed from the beginning by the God of the Bible.

We live in fact in a damaged world, just as the Bible lays out. Pain is real; suffering, whether of natural or human origin is widespread. But now we are given hope, we can acquire skills from sufficient information, and gain confidence knowing that God had something else in mind all along. Passive acceptance is neither useful nor redemptive. God Himself grieves over what happened to His creation. He actively works into it and wants to use human beings as agents to bring about very practical improvements in all of life.

For these reasons *economics* is not limited to the vast network of commerce in buying and selling things in markets; rather, it encompasses the whole effort to straighten out the house we live in and the lives we lead by every human activity.

The Importance of Moral Enterprise

The Bible calls for intelligent action, moral opposition and creative enterprise to stand up to frustration, injustice, poverty and even death. As we shall see, that is the call of God for each of us. We take our cue from ideas, not from what simply happens. We think and discern with our minds first and only then decide how to respond with our bodies. We have a calling to be human and impress on history that we have not bowed to destiny, false powers or an impersonal and unfair nature. God gave us a charge

---

3. Paul's letter to the Colossians, chapter 1:9ff.

The Case for Moral Opposition

to work, resist evil and repair our damaged world. We are exhorted to create a better environment where people in God's household and their neighbors can live and work together.

This is part of the broader cultural mandate in the Bible, the reasoning and compass for much of what is good and beneficial in protecting and furthering each life, body and soul. Of course the use of the same mandates in ways that disregard moral and factual restraints was often harmful and resulted in bad situations, laws and practices.

The Jewish Scriptures and the whole Christian Bible uniquely advocate creative work not simply as a way to survive, but at all times as a way to give shape and beauty to the world and bring love and justice into human relations. Economic benefits result in the reduction of hunger, idleness and oppression through the Bible's mandates to enrich every life creatively. We shall see later that the God introduced in the Bible worked "from the beginning"[4] with great determination and delight in details to create a good world. He made men and women in His image to carry on that activity with our own work and thereby honor, delight and obey Him.

The Bible gives one universal law, a governing rule of a rational universe, from which all details are mere extrapolations and applications. "The Great Commandment" to love God with all our heart, mind, soul and strength, and to love our neighbor as we love ourselves is not foreign to God; it describes His Being and character. It is the quasi-constitutional law of human existence. Any further exposition and rules are only illustrative applications of that constitution to clarify how people should understand it. All thought and activity should be an expression in practice of what loving God and fellow human being involves, and should be measured by that standard.

The Measure of a Personal Universe

Two things are central to this constitution or fundamental law of the universe. First, it points out that we live in a personal universe, not an impersonal one; personality is real in all eternity, prior to all matter or energy. Second, it points out that people have intrinsic value, no matter how rich or poor, beautiful or ugly, healthy or ill, skilled or needy. Their life, personality and ability to stand against death in any form must be our first concern.

---

4. Gen 1:1 and John 1:1 point out that "before the beginning" God existed and then acted to give to everything an original beginning.

Everyone deserves respect, education, food and shelter, and the protection of law against being exploited by other people or situations.

Later we shall consider what that implies in modern life. Regardless of how we choose to remember it, by a sign on our notice board or the memory in our minds and hearts, according to the common Jewish and Christian view, God has called us to get things done so that life is made more possible through acts of love and justice, and may be richer, more colorful and more fulfilling for everyone.

Call for Human Agency

That is of course only possible with a shift away from a fatalistic perspective, out of a closed system of cause and effect, to an open view of creative action into history. The God of the Bible intended that all of life's necessities, bread and drink for our bodies, shelter against the weather, and peace and order through law in the community be provided in each generation through the work of men and women. He created an open system and gave instruction to our minds to motivate our hearts about what is right and honorable. God gets things done through the agency of people; the earth provides, but things are made by human hands as human minds direct.

When skills are put to work and abilities are developed our personalities are enriched. Work reminds us that we are neither beasts nor angels: we depend on food and shelter for our bodies but we also have the power to transform nature into culture and make a human habitat. Work helps develop our self-esteem as we accomplish things well. Through work we also recognize our ability to help others[5] and become vehicles that genuinely affect the external world. With work we reflect the God in whose image we have been made as people.

This high view of persons from Christianity revolutionized people and societies over time, sensitizing them to recognize problems and seek solutions. Alternatives became an advantage rather than a threat to accepted views. The mind and thought gained importance, as did moral discernment and a desire to improve life. God's calling to individuals made everyone responsible, encouraging the personal autonomy necessary to bring about invention, subjectivity, originality and creative agency.

---

5. Eph 4:28; 2 Thess 3:8–12.

The quest for truth in any area, from ideas explored by early philosophers, for example in Greece and China, to the original art of writers and painters, from considering the nature of the real world to studying how to make things useful and easier, from enacting laws that prevent evil to the discovery of laws governing nature: all this and more freed people from bondage to fear, ignorance, exploitation and personal insignificance. We shall see in the next chapter that breaking fear is central to God's dealing with us. "Fear not" the angel announced to the shepherds. It is the same for anyone who sets out to exercise dominion by figuring out how an orderly creation works.

Chapter 3

Power Gained Through Knowledge

FOR MOST PEOPLE THE world appears as a complex and dangerous puzzle. We all experience a similar history throughout our childhood and into later years: reality is not simple, obvious, or comfortable, but gives a mix of diverse, colorful, comforting, and sometimes disquieting sensations. We experience pleasure as well as discomfort and pain; loneliness and insecurity are as real as love; unfair treatment and unpredictable reactions often follow the satisfaction that comes from loving attention and understanding. Real dangers, disappointments, and physical or emotional hurt threaten us on many sides. We manage to love and communicate, but often experience frustration, anxiety, and even bodily harm.

The first steps to make life more bearable and prosperous are to understand it, discover a larger purpose than just existing, and find ways to become as safe as possible. Such efforts are part of being human, of using our minds to distinguish mental and moral categories. It is the task of parents and teachers, government and neighborhoods, economists (as defined above), craftsmen, and philosophers to make that easier. Their efforts should help make life possible and enable everyone to have some success.

Security Through Knowledge

Safety in life, business, and community is achieved through the application of intelligent observational and manual skills and rational reflection that together help us manage all kinds of dangers, including the physical ones and those that arise from the way we think, what we believe, and how we understand the real world and ourselves. Mental and intellectual skills, such as the critical reasoning powers required to seek and discern good ideas, lead to an intelligent understanding of the natural world and of the power of ideas to shape behavior. They require personal, intellectual, and moral/practical discipline.

The better we understand something the less threatening it is to us. By learning skills we diminish problems and accept or diffuse challenges. Laws that define and mark what behavior is acceptable and what is not alert us to failures, inconsistencies, and other hidden or open ways in which life is not what it ought to be. Some laws *describe* regular events and others *prescribe* what paths to follow in order to diminish and even avoid damages.

Geography, cold and heat, rivers and ravines, and other natural conditions present physical danger. The earth may be flat and easily flooded or mountainous. Mudslides destroy more slowly than the earthquakes that suddenly shake things up. We will be safer when we know such things in order to adjust and improve the place we live and the protections we construct, the trees we plant and the foundations we lay.

Physical dangers also exist when people attack and overpower their neighbor and his belongings by force and crime, by trickery and deceit. People may offer help but they can also do great harm. In that way we are unpredictable, real choice-makers. Laws attempt to define acceptable behavior and appropriate punishment for violators in the hope of effectively influencing or altering their behavior.

A third source of physical danger is ignorance of the world we live in: some foods may be poisonous and some materials may be used inappropriately. Bacteria and viruses attack our vulnerable bodies when our defenses are broken down or simply weak. Improved skill and years of experience have diminished these dangers, but if knowledge does not grow and is not passed on to the next generation with accurate explanations, it is not really valued and will gradually be lost.

Discernment Before Belief

Just as great as physical dangers, if not more so, are those arising from insufficient or faulty beliefs about the real world of things, animals, and people. One may assume that things are correctly seen from habit or tradition, from living in a community of similar ideas. Shared collective thought gives the impression of accuracy: surely so many people can't be wrong!

However, group belief easily prevents healthy doubt about its own trustworthiness. When a view results from insufficient curiosity, questioning, and testing it remains an opinion that does not necessarily correspond to reality. Membership in the group can strengthen an otherwise inadequate belief because a community of like-minded people tends to make its members afraid to search for a better, more fitting answer to questions and doubts that arise in a dangerous world. Group authorities often do not appreciate either individual or external inquiry. The doubter outside the group's consensus is considered dangerous. The demand to work under a collective stifles individual creativity and prevents the open mind necessary to imagine unusual alternatives.

Both physical dangers and faulty views create a kind of bondage, a false sense of security based on obedience to the group instead of a more thorough understanding of life and reality. Marxist collective thinking and non-Biblical religious communities have both offered a sense of belonging, but no confidence that one can sleep in safety or be truthful to the demands of the real world. (Even within Christianity we find groups which frequently gave more weight to belief with a narrow focus than to knowledge enlarged through study, observation and careful considerations of what the Bible teaches us about life in the real world.)

Physical dangers are reduced when we take our heart into our hands and decide to develop greater skills and explore new alternatives. We run tests to make sure that our explanation or theory matches what is happening before our eyes or in our stomach. Such risk has two prerequisites: we must recognize our ignorance and be willing and eager to do something about it.

We reduce ignorance through skillful discovery, while knowledge is increased by means of education. Refusing to merely submit to the rules found in natural physical forces, we must seek to understand their causes and consequences, and how each relates to the others. We make use of them to serve us further. For this purpose we insist on building more solid houses, irrigating the dry land, wearing more effective clothes against the weather, and washing the dirt off our bodies. We observe the regular physical interaction of things by weight and volume, by distance in perspective; chemical reactions follow patterns we can use to our benefit. Already familiar with the old ways, we dare to find new ones that create greater safety. We gain distance and perhaps even a measure of independence from nature in pursuit of meeting human needs. We determine to know and thereby to exercise some control over our lives.

We can say then that a culture of life values individual people and encourages them to rule over primitive and unchallenged nature. Jews and Christians have always been invited, even commanded, to subdue the earth and have dominion over it by means of creativity, language, and practical know-how. They accept that part of our initial calling is to increase available understanding, to learn how things work and what can be done to both improve and embellish life. All of reality is open to our observation, study, and exploration as we find ways, through intelligent skills and moral/cultural choices, to alter what is otherwise merely present in nature.

All humans are connected to the earth through our bodies, but in our mind and purposes we are free from its dictates. Meaning is not derived from dumb, silent nature, which is impersonal and amoral, and shows us simply what is. Only the Jewish and Christian Bible tells Man not only what is, but also what ought to be and what could be both new and better.

Cultural Mandate

I use the term *culture* to describe more than song and dance, art and dress, customs and lifestyle. It does contain those things as minor, more anecdotal aspects, though that is all some people include in the definition. In my view culture is, however, much more. It centrally concerns how people orient their lives to the patterns of the natural world and act in response to what they believe about life and death, time and work, the individual and the group, authority and law, plus the possibility of real change.

The Bible's cultural mandates encourage people to create new and better ways. Nature's resources are turned into tools, fields grow food, and nature's sun gives light for work. People harness energy to break the dictates of night and darkness; water turns the wheel to power the mill, wind drives turbines to pump water for irrigation, waste is recycled for new products, and moral discernment solidifies into laws, so that justice demands appropriate and fair "ad-justment" respectful of each person.

That is how and why culture must shape nature, rather than the other way around.

We can, however, only consider changes in our way of life if we hold a high view of human beings. It should always really matter to us: human life is not defined by biology, history, or nature alone. Only when men and women understand their lives to be more than their bodies, more than a statistical appearance in history, and more than a part of an impersonal diversity of natural things will they dare to step out of the cycle of repetition and search for a safer, longer, easier, more contented and dignified life.

Many people believe that human beings came about by natural processes and forces. Together with all things and animals, they are subject to nature's forms, part of the *One*, and nothing encourages them to break traditional patterns, even if they are painful and hostile. Life is insecure from generation to generation, leading to low survival rates of children, short life spans for adults, exposure to the weather, to dismal conditions, powerful and bad rulers, and endless additional burdens. A life bound to such traditions manifests little respect for people and leaves them in untreated pain, fear, and uncertainty. Repeated complaints and tears cannot improve life as long as people see themselves totally and inescapably stuck in a cycle of unavoidable natural tragedies.[1]

Avoidable Tragedies

From my experience and perspective I consider these lives to be tragedies rather than simply a common outcome, because death is an obvious enemy, a contradiction to life, to the mind, and to qualities only human beings can exhibit. Resignation to death contradicts initiative, creativity, and moral discernment.

My perspective about death is formed by three considerations. I find most people share the same view, though they often express it in different ways. The first is that until very recent times people everywhere assumed that human life continues after death in some form. Burial customs, art works, tools, and food in gravesites demonstrate such an expectation throughout centuries of history.

Secondly, in the face of death all people are sad; they cry and lament the interruption of what they hoped would not end. Death is nowhere accepted as normal and timely, as just another part of human experience. It is always the end of a life shared with others in body and soul, an active mind, a life, whether wise or foolish, linked in conversation and relationships, a human person.

Thirdly, and distinct from other views, the Biblical view is that death is in no way part of God's original intention for human beings. There has

---

1. V.S. Naipaul vividly describes such views in *The Masques of Africa: Glimpses of African Belief* (Knopf, 2010). See especially the section on belief in Gabon.

been an historic break as a result of sin, disobedience, and a rejection of God. The fracture from what was there before is not an act of God, a part of nature, or a personal punishment, but a loss of the world into which people were created to live as human beings. Life and death are not two sides of the same coin; instead death is abnormal, a contradiction to life, and should be opposed through personal, moral, and intelligent efforts.

This unique Biblical teaching is also the justification for our efforts to regain dominion, to make the desert bloom, to confront the injustice of rulers and employers, to establish the rule of law for all people, both weak and strong, and to fight as much for life as against death, with reason and by means of science and technology. The charge to deliberately plough the fields for food[2] rather than to gather what one casually finds lying about is added to the earlier mandate to subdue the earth and have dominion.

In most other cultures human death has always been accepted as part of the normal life cycle from birth to death, even though this customary response is contradicted by tears. Traditions assume normality, so they maintain and repeat familiar patterns of response. Communal stories recount what has always been and must never change. The role assigned to people is that of a ball kicked around by the universe, by cosmic forces, by spirits and gods. Fear obliges each generation to fear again, to submit, and to attempt to appease through sacrifice, self-abasement, and denial, thereby removing all motivation and any hope of change.

Two images come to mind to illustrate the difference: the obedient guardian of the master's house silently dusts the furniture, while the economist constantly thinks and works to improve and embellish his dwelling and that of his community.

The Enterprising Mind

The second picture illustrates how the Bible encourages enterprise rather than continued repetition, admiration and the maintenance of the status quo. We are called to resist both blind repetition and death in any of its forms. In other words, from a concern for human beings and their safety, we should take suffering and complaints about life more seriously and decide to do something about them, rather than accepting endless recurrence of what has been the case for so long.

---

2. Gen 4:18ff and 1:28.

We need to oppose cultures of repetition, to review our own inherited and ingrained cultural habits and improve on them to enhance security and the possibility of a fuller life now and in the future through reasoned, determined, practical efforts. Prosperity means "forward looking"; it is not a gift, but a reward to those who look ahead and create a way to get there.

Jewish and Christian teaching creates a mindset that embraces a culture of improvement, innovation, and personal initiative. The Bible answers the basic questions about who *Man* is, both male and female, what use we should make of our *minds*, and what the *meaning* of it all is to us individually. God tells us that we are wanted and loved and encourages us to create better lives. In that light we can stand up against the dictates of the past wherever they do not serve us well.

The past outlook may have kept us wounded, enslaved, humiliated, and ignored. But now we embrace a culture of creation, of work and effort towards mastery of circumstances. We must learn to discern and reject the traditions of nomads, hunters, and gatherers who depended on nature's impersonal presence, gleaning only what was found on the surface of the landscape, and never looking beneath it for treasures. They rarely scratched the surface, much less ploughed and fertilized the land to make it produce. But now we may choose to embrace a culture of creation and work towards mastery of our circumstances.

Change starts with what happens in the mind, in the world of ideas. There, in our thoughts, we review what we have done and what alternatives might be possible. Only in the mind do we first recognize a problem and imagine a solution. Only in the mind can we compare what we now know with what might be an improvement and what we can learn from others. For example, farmers learned that animal power could replace human effort to scratch the soil for planting seeds; a steel plough turns the soil deeper than a wooden one; a motor vehicle to pull it is even more efficient. We do not embrace the cycle from food to human waste by drinking our own urine. Instead we dig some distance away for a source of water that is filtered through sand and gravel. We rotate crops and improve storage. We refine skills and admit weakness or failure, keeping our minds open for improvements.

We will be loved and respected when we ourselves readily go out of our way to consider the needs of others, love them, and lend a hand to diminish their hardship. We can begin to help others when we no longer accept our own experiences, or theirs, as always fair, deserved, and inevitable or unchangeable.

You will remember that I suggested above how important it is not only to be born a human being, but also to *become* one by developing and using our minds[3]. For each situation demands a cultivated life of the mind to imagine alternatives, shapes, and pictures of hoped-for worlds. That is what the Bible provides through its accounts, stories and poems, laws and proverbs. All good literature responds with parallel accounts of the varieties of human existence. Every text addresses us with ideas and information in the form of concepts expressed in grammatical sentences and a rich, descriptive vocabulary, with links to real experiences.

More Than Meets the Eye

New ideas present a fuller circle of life than what is already apparent in our limited experience. We read of a larger world than our own: good and bad governments, faithful and deceitful spouses, hardships and blessings, opportunities wasted and chosen, and the great variety of ways people work and make a living. The novelty and diversity of these human situations, in addition to what the Bible tells of God's presence and care, enrich and enable us to seek open alternatives to any narrowly circumscribed existence.

It is not surprising that the cultures informed by the Bible as a text for the mind, a text that explains, challenges, critiques, and informs human beings, exhibit great freedom and respect for individuals, and have successfully improved human existence in many different ways. With the knowledge of another way of life people have been freed from the bondage of submission to local habits, authoritarian rulers, gods, spirits, kings or even, at times, disrespectful husbands and shrewish wives!

As soon as we do this we begin to address the second source of fear, mentioned above. I will discuss this in the next chapter.

---

3. Willard Gaylin's *Adam and Eve and Pinocchio: On Being and Becoming Human*.

Chapter 4

You May Need to "Check Your Glasses"

THE SECOND KIND OF fear arises when beliefs about the central areas of life do not sufficiently affect our ability to cope with and master our fragile existence. In other words, there are beliefs that have little grounding in real life and prevent us from finding out what that life consists of and why it is this way. Such beliefs are often strongly held, but are mostly based on superstition imposed erroneously on reality. Instead of seeing a situation in the light of reasonable and verifiable information, superstition keeps a person in darkness about what is true. The result is an inaccurate reading of reality, part fear and part imagination, based on assumptions without regard to facts. At worst, these beliefs are an expression of deep fear without any reference at all to the real world. They are the stuff of which magic and fairy tales are made.

Fears arise not only from actual dangers, from accidents and hardships in our world such as floods and landslides, earthquakes and fire, but also from ignorance about the nature of things which surround us. Similar ignorance often exists about materials used incorrectly for a given job; when the physical limits and chemical reactions of materials are not known, terrible things can happen. Bridges need to carry the load crossing them. Walls have to hold up the roof and withstand wind and weather. Glue has to bind enough for the required strength, and welding needs to be done with the necessary heat for specific metals to bond.

Such fears, whether from lack of factual knowledge or from superstitious thinking, are in need of urgent correction to better address a world that is not harmonious or benevolent, but dangerous. Fear originates in a person's own mindset. In an unfriendly human or natural setting it may not be baseless and unjustified; it can even be a helpful tool.[1] Learning and remembering how things function lead to increasing mastery of material things and the reduction of fear.

However, we also need to recognize that when fear is part of our way of thinking about the real world, it is a fear created by us in our minds. Reality is steady, not random or capricious, and therefore lawful. Therefore, if our belief is not accurate about the nature and form of the world, then our perception must adjust and change through our own effort. Fear too often results from unexamined belief, plain ignorance, and what are in fact inappropriate and false interpretations and obligations. Because we want everyone to agree, we insist they also accept false views that can not make the unknown known or replace ignorance with discernment and insight. Thus fear is maintained for generations.

Religious teachers and politicians may be equally at fault here. It is as if they force everyone to look through warped lenses, creating a common distorted vision that replaces reality. Propaganda phrases, repeated in unison, accomplish the same thing, when government posters declare that there is enough food in North Korea or that Israel planted sharks along Egypt's coasts to destroy its tourist industry: something is held forth as true when in fact its appeal lies in group repetition. The volume of noise and frequency of repetitions has become more important than substance.

Reality Corrects Our Vision

We all start our life believing our view of the world is accurate. But, as a young boy, when I began to fall over roots in the path, missed the height of the curb, and poured liquid next to the glass instead of into it, I found that this was a mistaken belief. My eyes no longer gave me a view I could live with. I realized I needed corrective lenses, eyeglasses, because I had gradually become nearsighted. Only corrective glasses could put reality back into the proper perspective, helping me to avoid those embarrassing and often painful mistakes.

People who do not want to see reality accurately do not wear glasses. They may consider them a handicap, but only create more problems by

---

1. It is a good choice to be afraid of a raging bull, a poisonous snake, a suspicious stranger, at times a politician or even a medical doctor. I always check the credentials and competence of the latter. The former I argue with to receive more than charming phrases.

their choice. They may even shut their eyes altogether, but then they will always stumble. Others wear colored glasses to create a false view of the real world simply because they prefer it that way. Glasses that change what you see, either sharper or more blurred, represent the way you understand what happens around you, either by inheritance or by choice.

What glasses do you wear? How do you know that you see the real world rather than an interpretation from personal fears or desires, parents, traditions, or ruling authorities that want you to believe things regardless of whether they are true to reality? How would you know, unless you critically examine what you have been told?

Moving from a culture of repetition to one of innovation is a change from fear to daring, from the relative comfort experienced in communal pain and thinking it normal, to recognizing that it is abnormal and struggling to find another way, because you decide that it is abnormal compared to what you struggle for in life all along.

Since you can imagine alternatives you should think them through to their consequences.

Let's try that using the following reflections. Are there natural impersonal things without minds of their own that influence you, like stones, water, trees, and dirt[2] or are these the hostile work of deities, spirits, nasty neighbors, or other enemies? Think this through and consider alternatives in your mind. You will differentiate in your responses. Impersonal things you can change or move away; if they are animated, you fear their strength from personal weakness, and tend to do nothing.

Next, consider the following. If you see human beings as just a part of nature you will most likely accept what you experience. If, on the other hand, you recognize that only persons think, talk, and imagine, you will realize that silent, uncaring nature can not be the real home or origin of human beings who are so different from it. Nature binds every natural thing in its embrace. The only alternative is a thinking, working, and loving creator who alone could have made us distinctly as we are. No one has ever come up with another adequate explanation for human personality and freedom, when everything around us is bound and impersonal.

---

2. In the film "Out of Africa" the foreman says that rain water should not be kept behind a dam, but allowed to run away, for "it wants to live in Mombassa." Does water express a desire, or does the force of gravity pull always to the lowest point?

The Nature of Our Universe

Let's pursue this argument in reverse. Since something exists here now, in our lifetime, there must always have been something existing; nobody has observed or suggests that something can come out of truly nothing. We do not observe a spontaneous creation anywhere. Consequently something has to have always been. If the "stuff" that always existed is impersonal energy or matter, you and I are misfits, for we are persons, something odd in a world of impersonal forces. If, on the other hand, there is a personal Being who thinks, feels, acts, and loves, who is called God, we are at home in the world because we also think, feel, act, and love.

But is this personal God also good? If you look at life as normal, you are likely to assume that everything has to be the way it always has been. You may weep, but there is nothing to be done about it. However, if you decide that life is possibly abnormal you can set out to change and correct it according to an standard not defined by what is common or usual. That standard may be unknown to you now, but you may begin to wonder whether and how it can be discovered.

If you believe that life and death are natural and equal simply because they happen all the time, you will hardly investigate ways to prolong, improve, and value life and fight death, even though death amounts to a cruel contradiction to life and everyone complains about it. What justifies our complaint? Is the refusal to accept death passively just another impersonal event, an item in a statistic?

If you believe we live in a lawful universe, because the sun always rises, clouds bring rain in regular patterns, water always runs downhill, where trees only ever bear their own fruit, and people only ever give birth to little human beings you would still see that human beings are often unpredictable. You would have to conclude that what human beings formulate into laws, maintain as traditions, and embrace as power structures, in contrast to the fixed laws of nature, cannot all be true, wise, and legitimate. You would realize from your own behavior that we all contradict ourselves frequently, make false accusations, use words both to inform and to misinform, and lie for our own benefit. That should make you think about the difference between the same just laws for everyone and laws that only maintain the powers that rule over you.

Alternatively, some people believe that their life is controlled by capricious spirits or people and therefore live in great fear. Conflicts impose many undeserved burdens on their lives and constantly make them victims of the larger, hidden circumstances. You will attempt to appease them without ever being sure of reaching that goal, seeking help from 'special' people like mystics, shamans, medicine men, or witches, who claim to know the secret mysteries, to have hidden knowledge about how to manipulate or disarm counter-forces for a price. Both good and bad events suggest a chaotic, invisible realm of competing spirits that inhabit nature and turn human beings into victims of their games.

Making Sense of Reality

Many people around the world see life in this superstitious way. With no central confidence in reason, order, and justice this view nurses no certainty, discouraging all consistent dominion over life, work, and society. It is like being in charge of a house without a lock on the door, where disruptive people come and go randomly and dirt and dust make every effort to keep order vain. It is impossible to be economical in and make sense of that situation.

The alternative is to discover a fundamental reason underlying all reality. The laws governing things are accessible to careful trial and observation; there is order, a unity of power, and lawfulness. When you observe regular patterns and discover valid, consistent definitions, and the rules by which natural things function, such knowledge gives you confidence and reduces fear of the unknown; you can then anticipate and plan ahead. The orderliness of natural life suggests one fundamental law for all, and if a person with a mind is at the origin of it, that person must have a dependable character, neither playing games at your expense, nor hiding in mystery.

Even humans have their own order and predictability, not as biological or material machines, but because we can always count on their untidy actions to be unpredictable. We can never assume to know anyone's next step or decision. Humans are an open system, possessing a measure of sovereignty and the power to originate thoughts and actions. That makes us something more than "natural" as we think and choose, complain and create. Only human beings consciously notice the unpredictable choices other people make. Both by definition and in our experience they complain and fear, pose a puzzle to one another, but also seek knowledge, satisfaction, and joy.

You May Need to "Check Your Glasses"

That is the sovereign perch from which we make the distinction between what is normal and what is abnormal, what should be and what should not be, and from which we set to work.

Just as we move to higher ground when floods threaten, so too we must move our mental image of reality to a different intellectual level to avoid the rising tide of an impersonal nature in order to develop a culture of life, work, and profitable enterprise.

Safety in an unsafe world must be achieved both intellectually and physically, by a change in our beliefs and subsequent behavior. If we do not ever consider this a possible necessity, we will always remain in our older patterns, subjected to mixed experiences that include much pain, frustration, and fear.

A shift to higher ground in our mental landscape requires that we take a first step out of our usual and hitherto common ways of thinking and doing. Only then are we taking our pain seriously and acting on it. For pain and complaint function as teachers, informing us of unacceptable conditions and telling us to seek solutions. This is the first step to greater safety.

Another way of seeing this is to imagine moving into an empty house. You gradually furnish it with the things you need, want, and will remember later; in the same way you furnish your mind and memory with what you see and experience. Your mental house then becomes more than just a location, it becomes a home. It is now a place where you are "at home," surrounded by ideas, insights, and purposes which will provide memories and possibly nurture a growing family. Through increasing insight, you gain the confidence to manage many of the challenges of your world. You understand events in context and anticipate challenges with reasonable confidence, knowing what is possible and what requires further help.

Such a move to higher ground with its greater security first took place many centuries or millennia ago when people insisted that Nature, the sun and moon, the seasons of the year, and the cycles of fertility were not our ancestors or what made us human. In contrast to Egyptian or Babylonian religions, the Bible tells of a people who believed instead that a God in heaven, invisible but present, an eternal being with characteristics of personality, and provided explanations accessible to the reasonable mind. He made human beings distinct from impersonal nature and in his image.

The Bible opens the door to seeing reality in a unique way, free from the distorting filters of religious faith which human imagination so frequently creates. From the beginning the biblical emphasis is on central propositions to be examined, which remove the Bible from the category of a religious book to one of teachings and explanations. Instead of rituals, there are words in whole texts that invite discovery and increased knowledge. God asks us to believe first on the level of the mind, i.e. our sharp and critical comprehension and evaluation of the connection between text and reality, and then to believe on the level of chosen action, to carry out what is right, good, and just in a much damaged history.

A Contract Between God and Man

The text from God, the content of the Bible's teaching, is addressed to each individual as a distinct person with a critical mind. It is a text about facts, in grammatical form and in sentences that require being read, debated, and understood like any other text. Much of it is in the form of a contract or covenant. It is not a challenge or an invitation to a collective, a village, or a nation, but to each person individually. God, who makes a covenant, a binding contract between partners, takes each of us seriously and gives a sealed commitment of his favor, love, and promise. Partners in a contract of this nature forgo the mentality of fear and submission; God is tied to his promises by virtue of his character, and Man is committed to faithfully honor his calling as a human being. The same standards apply to both God and Man. They can argue with each other, set out reasons for their points, and demand compliance.

This covenant or contract is part of a linear outlook to life, a history in which the future is different from the present and the past, a progressive move towards a fuller life. Efforts will have results. Things and circumstances can be improved. Personal significance, for better and for worse, is established and rewarded.

Many propositions are unique to this contract, among them the weekly reminder from the Sabbath command that human beings are unlike everything else in the universe. Like God, so too Man takes a day of rest to distance human life from the routines of nature in their undifferentiated and uninterrupted daily patterns. The Sabbath rest confirms a fundamental freedom from nature's model and offers a life governed by choice, not controlled by repetition.

The seeds for a Jewish/Christian view of life, culture, and dominion lie in this and other unique propositions, as we shall see. Believers are given the respect due to adults in their mastery over the impoverishing performance of fate and the fearsome ignorance of people who have never heard of the God of the Bible. We have the right and privilege to collaborate alongside God in work, life, and society.

Abraham's Belief

Abraham believed and accepted that covenant almost 4000 years ago in the large city of Ur in Mesopotamia, which is modern Iraq, where he traded and raised a family.[3] But in his mind, with his convictions and ethical outlook, he lived as one who, unlike his neighbors, believed in the real existence of one personal and good God in heaven. Only God's character and being could explain all of natural life and the distinctiveness of personal human existence. So Abraham left the culture and pattern of life that surrounded him, becoming the first in a long line of individuals who reject the religious views of those among whom they live.

In the surrounding Babylonian society people believed that the sun and moon, the seasons of the year, the flood cycles of the Tigris and Euphrates rivers, and the powers behind the fertility of the land controlled their lives. They worshipped many deities like "Sin" represented by the Moon, "Shamash" by the Sun, and Baal's consort "Ishtar" (a name that surfaces again in Germanic languages as the word "star" or "Stern"). Babylonians believed the divine presences they perceived in nature, with everyone sharing the same outlook and practice. Nature bound them into its cycles of seed time and harvest, life and death, and the endless rotation of sun and moon.[4]

For Chaldeans there was no real God in heaven, only many powers behind natural events. Abraham understood reality very differently. He knew that things are things; trees and rivers, the sun and the moon, are just that: creations and nothing more. But he also knew a person as creator: he believed that only one possible God could answer the many questions of existence.

The difference between persons and things, the rule of one authority in an orderly natural world, a conflict-riddled human world of contradictory life experiences, the contrast between the joy of birth and the sorrow over death, and the significance of human choice to reach "higher ground":

3. Gen 12:1ff.
4. Zeph 1:5ff and Jer 8:2 complain against a similar tendency among later Israelites.

all that is only reasonable in light of what Abraham believed from God and why he trusted God to have told the truth to a long line of his ancestors, to Adam, to both Cain and Abel, Noah, and all the generations in between. The personal, thinking, rational God in heaven addressed their minds in the concepts which language forms, rather than through their senses, whether through the eyes and ears, the stomach, or sexuality.

The entire Bible fleshes out this contrast to nature religions and makes it more explicit. God communicates in language to help us discern with our minds, not our bodies, what is good, true, and right. The focus is on making sense rather than on sensual feelings.

Paul taught the same in the church in Thessalonica soon after Jesus' death and resurrection.[5] And everywhere into our own time, when people apply what Abraham and Paul believed and taught, we find continuity in outlook and similar results: freedom from fear and an encouragement to be active human beings, an educated and enlightened effort to fight evil and the suffering of people in their self-imposed condition as victims of circumstances. The God of the Bible allows people to banish all spirits and deities called forth in the fear and weakness of the human imagination.

God Is Not At Home in Nature

Religious constructions of nature deities are easy to imagine and pursue. Their origin seems to make sense initially when people live with few resources in harsh landscapes and rough weather. People are also left without an intellectual recourse by the painful and inhuman cruelty of others who, in their arrogance, control, exploit, or neglect neighbors in times of need. Both natural and social problems burden our minds and bodies with their power.

Beliefs of a religious or ideological nature originate in the mind, from inside one's own way of thinking; we alone are to blame. Any belief of a religious or ideological nature can keep us from seeing and recognizing a wider world: natural resources that remain hidden, medical care not pursued, answers to questions never asked. We miss out because we do not look for what is needed. Belief in the normality of all events, that they have to occur, keeps people from imagining alternatives. We will hardly look for solutions if we fail to recognize problems or even the possibility of something being a problem. Nothing will change when neither

---

5. 1 Thess 1:9–10.

an alternative nor a solution is imaginable, when it is assumed that we deserve whatever is thrown into our path.

Our belief can keep us from developing the greatest resource we have, which is the human mind, our passion for knowledge, our capacity for love. Fear of the extra effort required, possible failure, or the judgment and laughter of neighbors, may keep us from looking for better ways to address life's many frustrations. Poor hygiene, sickness, and poverty, lack of punctuality, ignorance, and the failure to love should never be accepted as inevitable, necessary, or final.

Paul's teaching turned former victims of circumstance and the caprice of Greek gods into agents of change. With a more biblical view of life, under one true and living God, believers began to change their social habits and work practices.[6] They questioned unjust authorities and slowly transformed corrupt societies into ones governed by the rule of the same law for everyone. They encouraged education and respect for people, stood up to autocrats that ruled with cruelty, and comforted people who were socially outcast because they were different. For the first time men widely respected women as equals. Free people took up work to exhibit their unique personalities and insights.

These changes result from the command to love God, rather than to remain ignorant or afraid, and then to love our neighbor as ourselves, doing unto others what we want done to ourselves.

What a God it must be, who tells us to love ourselves and the unique person in each neighbor![7] And what a difference it makes when the Bible presents a God who alone tells us that Man and Woman are equally made in God's image to be a help to each other! That is unique in the whole world and foreign to other religions and political ideologies.[8]

Abraham believed and Paul taught that one God alone is the only possible explanation of how the real world functions.[9] Many gods only lead to rivalry, struggle, and disruption, the opposite of loving God and loving people. In cultures without biblical insight Abraham and Paul experienced little love, much mistrust, and fear. Rival gods do not create an orderly and lawful world; they demand submission but do not present or argue a case for trust and mutual commitment.

6. 1 Thess 4:1–13.

7. Lev 19:18; Matt 5:43; 22:39; Rom 13:9.

8. Gen 3:16 is not a command, but a lament over the malpractice that after sin became powerful men will rule over women.

9. Exod 20:1ff.

By contrast, the God of the Bible addresses our minds with verifiable, accurate information linked to history and the shape of the real world. He makes his case sensibly because he wants to be understood, not followed blindly. He makes no demand for stupid obedience as an expression of our humility and deference to authority. We are invited to argue with God in order to improve our understanding.[10] Knowing something truthfully is better than believing simply because everyone else does.

The God of the Bible is the true and living God because he created human life in addition to common biology. He acts in history, shows emotions such as joy, compassion, laughter,[11] and sadness; he judges, and at times reveals his power in miracles. He sent prophets to explain what is good and right about all of life when people had forgotten and taught otherwise. He came to share a meal with Abraham and renew his promise to repair this damaged creation.[12] When the Son of God received a human body from a virgin's womb, becoming a real human person, he could address the underlying problem that had caused the damage: Jesus paid with his death for our guilt of unbelief and disobedience, and then overcame death powerfully in a real resurrection of the body.[13]

Paul points out that this living God helps us see history in a linear direction.[14] Things and events will not always repeat themselves, like a closed circle or the wheel of fate, the ocean tides or the movement of celestial bodies in the firmament above us. Instead, history and our lives move toward a goal. No one is replaceable by someone else. Every day will be new, unlike the one before, and every choice will have a lasting effect. History proceeds and we walk in it with new decisions, taking steps to improve the human situation. The Bible calls us to a life of enterprise and constructive work, to earn a living, and to create a just and lawful society. Only if life carries on after death is the investment in life before death of real and lasting significance. For then nothing is lost, wasted, and futile. In the Biblical perspective, every good action and choice will add to a foundation that nothing and no one can take away.

Paul writes that when the goal towards which all history moves is reached, all pain, injustice, sorrow, and fear shall be removed. God, who

---

10. Moses, Job, Jeremiah, and Jesus each views the difficulty of their situation and argues with God about it.

11. Ps 2.

12. Gen 3:15 and 18:1–15.

13. 1 Cor 15; last chapters of all four Gospels.

14. 1 Thess 1:10.

made the world and raised Jesus from the dead, has not finished his work. We can expect him to make all things new and to defeat all forms of death. At some time in a historic future there will be a restored world without problems, without sin and its power. Death shall be done away with, it will be no more. There is life after death, because Jesus gave evidence of that already in his own resurrection. He did not turn into a spirit or only remain alive in the disciples' thoughts. He had lunch[15] with them and showed himself many times to more than 500 witnesses[16] before his ascension.[17] Death is not the end; Jesus is alive now, and he will one day come again to reign and to make all things whole.

When death is not the final event, but superseded by a creative life without end, life here and now is worth a fight. We seek justice now in anticipation of what God will accomplish in fullness later. The work of every doctor, teacher, lover, or business entrepreneur expresses, in bits and parts, what God will sooner or later make perfect.

The whole Bible confirms Paul's words: we live in a moral world under a judge, not an impersonal world of forces and mere power structures. What happens today is not necessarily right and just, and there will be a day of reckoning when everything and every person will be judged. Neither nature, traditions, nor worldly rulers, are freed from future evaluation and judgment. Everything is being observed and nothing that is now wrong will be overlooked. With the promise and expectation of eventual justice from, God, no unfair powers and exploitive situations will have the last word. Those who have imprisoned people through false ideas and inhuman practices will be exposed. We are responsible to and cared for by a good, true, and living God who is eager to assist and fight for us.

There is then a comprehensive and truthful law for every aspect of the universe. That law is not a religious orientation from the Bible, but rooted in God's unchanging, lawful character. Since he made a lawful world, his law corresponds to the real world. The reason men and woman, for example, are equally human is not part of a religious point of view, which varies among people, but a factual and invariable observation. The fact that every person is born from a woman determines our perspective, rather than our individual and/or religious perspective that may, and often does, lead to a distortion of the facts. The weight of reality

15. John 21:8–14.
16. 1 Cor 15:6.
17. Acts 1:3ff.

speaks louder than any religious or ideological belief not linked to the critical facts on the ground.

In a moral world under God there are absolute definitions of right and wrong, true and false, fact and illusion. In a lawful world under God scientific insights flow from regular rather than random processes. Serious societies base their civil and criminal laws on definitions anchored in the character of God himself, supported by the evidence and shape of the real world and how it functions. These laws do not create a behavioral shape to society, but seek to express in statutes what prevents misbehavior. For example, many of the commandments are negations, for the avoidance of evil and destructive practices.

In following this discussion, you will understand that freedom from fear is rooted in the Bible's point of view and why fear is still so widespread where people have not understood it. Its information gives us knowledge and confidence The ideas found there encourage us to develop physical skills, mastery of products, and market possibilities. The Bible's ideas will always bear such fruit and transform any cultural context. They are not bits and pieces repeated fanatically from private reasoning, piety, devotion, or religious conviction. Their credibility comes from their self-evident and beneficial effect to remove the fear we all experience without God's better insight into a lawful creation of treasured individuals in the one human race.

God, after all, is the one who created the world and us in it. He is the only witness of that creation and can therefore tell us that all the pain and destruction resulting from the sin of Adam and Eve are not part of his original plan, but should be opposed.

This outlook encourages us all to stand up to a dangerous world and escape permanent victimhood. The Bible lays out an understanding of reality that supports every effort to raise human beings, with their minds and bodies, above what they find naturally around them. This calling is from God; we live neither at the mercy of a silent, impersonal, and often cruel nature, nor in a world haunted by capricious spirits and uncontrolled powers.

Discernment in a Messy World

According to the Bible we live in a world made by a definite God who truly exists. Intellectually there is no viable alternative explanation for this world of things and people. God tells us that he wanted not only things but also persons, that he loves us and is eager to tell us how we can be less insecure, fearful, and despondent. He tells us to look at life from the dual perspective of *necessary discernment* and of the *abnormality* of much of what happens.

Discernment requires the critical distance to look into the face of life and mark genuine distinctions. It sets us free from the temptation to neglect or abandon our individuality and critical faculties, our specific role as persons, by submitting to whatever happens anyway, by joining others in a group collective or to accept all things as necessary and inevitable. The recognition of abnormality liberates us from the idea that everything that happens is meant to happen, whether events in nature or through people's cruelty or kindness. We live in the fundamental unfairness of a fallen, abnormal and therefore dangerous world. Life's experiences, especially the contrasting obscenity of death to life, demand the openness to question, to argue, and to sort out what is right and good. *Discernment* helps us figure out which is which; the recognition of *possible abnormality* liberates us to make moral judgments. We must refuse to bow to pain, death, unfairness, ill health, and exploitive rulers.

In the next section I will lay out what I consider the stage instructions set out in the Bible in order to demonstrate more clearly their influence on our world of thought and practice. These instructions present the theme God had in mind when he first made an impersonal world and then put persons into it to bear his image. Human beings are intended to have dominion as God's agents over it.

Chapter 5

Someone There Before it All Began

WE HAVE ALREADY SEEN that from start to finish the language of the Bible carries a unique content. It appeals to people because it requires no secret key, no long preparation, no drugs or ecstasy, no abandonment of rational thought, or embrace of alternative criteria of inquiry. It contains no religious formulations or secret insights. It simply declares, as a proposition to be weighed and considered, that before anything existed at all there already was someone who thought, used his mind and power, and then decided to make what we know as heaven and earth, or in other words, everything.[1]

That proposition explains how human beings acquired their unique identity as persons who think, act, and feel, who imagine, decide, and create. We have a measure of sovereignty in a world in which everything else follows a closed natural program of necessary, i.e. not freely chosen, relationships. A world without humans is a world reduced to the pushes and shoves of chemistry and physics into the smallest details.

Outside of the Bible's declaration of God's eternal personal existence all other explanations of origins start with an impersonal something. Earlier I said that since "truly nothing" cannot bring about anything; a really existing world must have an eternal continuity of something. There is no possible alternative to either energy or a person having been there forever as the antecedent of what we now encounter.

No one has ever suggested how something can come out of truly nothing! Everyone assumes that "nothing" must be something. But "nothing" nothing does not end up being something!

---

1. Gen 1:1. The phrase "in the beginning" is repeated when Jesus is introduced in John 1:1.

Naturalists agree that some form of energy is the eternal source of everything in the real world. That could be the case, except that it does not explain how people turned out uniquely different from everything else, with freedom, choice, significance, language, and responsibility. We do not notice such abilities in things, plants, or animals which each follow a tight pattern of inter-*reactive* development and behavior.

People are simply different: besides having bodies made of matter and energy, we are also persons. Unlike a closed system of natural chains of transmission of information, human beings originate doubt, decisions, ideas, value judgments, and arguments. Energy or some pre-existing matter or dust cannot produce personality. A closed system cannot bring forth the openness assumed in real choices. The only remaining option is that we are the result of personality rather than matter. Only an eternally existing person could by choice produce energy and also other choice-makers. Our personality is then not a freak event, but derived from an eternally existing person.

That is the proposition with which the Bible begins. Personality is real in God forever and in human beings since their first creation. It is not the result of a process, but original. The rest of the Bible, all the way to the book of Revelation, in many different historic situations,[2] uses the grammar of real language in a variety of forms (such as explanations, lectures, poetry, sermons and historical records) to elaborate, illustrate, and clarify that the eternal thinking and acting person is God. In his Being, not just on occasion, he is love, full of generosity and grace, purposefully devoted to his creation and busily at work again, after the day of rest from all creation, to repair the damage incurred when the first two people messed things up by their false and foolish belief.[3]

Creation, One Day At a Time.

This central proposition of the Bible lays the groundwork for a delightfully detailed narrative of God's many sequential decisions that provide the context for all human existence. It tells us that the world came into being by someone's personal choice, and how we should look at it, work in it and how to be good persons. It is of little wonder then, that out of the Bible's teaching springs deep celebration and concern for human

2. Observe the work of the prophets and the record of the early church in Acts.
3. Gen 3:6.

beings, for the life of individuals, and for the human rights to life, health, property, and the security of the law's protection.

It is well worth our patience to think through how the Bible constructs that stage on which all of life is realized.

The first thing to notice is the delight and care with which God created this real world outside him, as a "vis-a-vis." By that I mean that creation does not exist in the mind of God, nor is God somehow contained in creation. The universe is not an extension of God. Each is in the presence of the other, but they are distinct. No other explanation ever justified, encouraged or demanded such respect for people in their individual personhood and for the natural world as already belonging to someone.

As we look at the developing scene in the early chapters of the Bible we understand the source of so much that we value in human life and work, plus the need to resist evil and its effects: social breakdown, violations of human rights, neglect of the natural world, and the demeaning demands of so many religions and political systems. The Bible nurtures in us a continuous pleasure in our exercise of dominion, as well as in our critique of imperfection through the pursuit of justice and honor for all of the image bearers of the Bible's God.

We immediately notice that at each distinct moment of time God is pleased with what he made.[4] Creation, and our part in it, is neither only a thought in his mind nor a part of himself; it is real and outside of God. He can and does look at it, because it is not a part of him.[5] Creation neither makes God larger nor emanates from him; it is made of things that can be changed, worked on, and differently organized and arranged. The distinct things in creation are not finished products once and for all, to be put into a museum for safe-keeping.

That description indicates that God took time to create. There is a sequence to his work that shows a development from idea to reality, from general to particular, and from raw material to intended product. Each period of work leads to greater differentiation and specificity as things become increasingly detailed. God did not accomplish everything in one act, but worked, shaped, and refined what he made. The Bible's account expresses delight in variety, richness of imagination, satisfaction with what is accomplished, and purposeful enjoyment of what everything became.

4. Gen 1:4, 10, 12, 18, 25, 31.
5. Gen 1:7, 11, 17, 24.

It is very important to understand the significance of this. It makes all the difference in our approach as human beings to human history where life, family, community, and business unfold. In the Bible God is not described as power, but as a person; not authoritarian, but authority. He thinks and acts in sequence, with a real difference between what was before and then after; this implies a sequential dynamic, a real history of serious considerations on the part of God. The first "something" of creation is divided into ever more specific and distinct things: day and night,[6] oceans and clouds,[7] water and land,[8] vegetation,[9] heavenly bodies, and animated creatures that swim, walk, and fly.[10] All these are part of a natural world made by God in distinct, deliberate, satisfying acts of creation.

Pleasure to God's Orderly Mind

The reason the creation of the world is described in this way is found in the nature of the God of the Bible: a single, eternal, and personal God with relationships between each member of the Godhead.[11] They love, think, and create together as they enjoy one another, all of which takes time: a give and take, a consideration of the others, and a pleasure in their relationship.[12] That is part of the nature of the God who created our world. Love, thought, pleasure, and creativity in a flow of time, in a real history, are the normal experiences of God by us and of each person in the Godhead.[13]

The satisfaction we crave lies in these realities. They describe what we desire and what fulfills us, the good life. Our craving of such realities

6. Gen 1:3–5.
7. Gen 1:6–8.
8. Gen 1:9–10.
9. Gen 1:11–13.
10. Gen 1:20–25.
11. This unique understanding of what people traditionally call "The Trinity" is a singular answer to the practical and philosophic question concerning the unity and diversity in all of life, allowing for form and freedom in language, real unity and genuine diversity between people of one human race, between particulars of the same species, etc.
12. It is the father's will; "From before the foundation of the world"; the love of Father for the Son. (John 17:23).
13. Consider the suggestion that God is outside physical, created time, but exists in timely sequence in his relationships and experiences, as developed in my book *The Innocence of God* (Paternoster, 2007).

is not hubris, but a normal and acceptable outlook on all of life, from family closeness to relations in business, between parents and children or management and workers, as well as between people and the world around them.

When the Bible states that God made things "according to their kind" we are instructed that everything has a definition, a form and fashion of its own from its first appearance. Things are not chaotically variable, exposed to genuinely random occurrences, but serve a purpose and can be relied on to perform what their kind can do. We live in a stable universe, the result of a rational God who created steadily performing things. Fact and process can be discovered and reliably used. We can return in the morning to what we left behind in the laboratory, or as a deposited promise in someone's mind, the night before. The universe has not turned into a different one overnight or from one generation to the next. Therefore, materials in our hands can be expected to maintain their composition and quality over time. Each kind of wood, stone, or metal can best serve a specific purpose.

God's character is also reflected in the lawful, rational, steady definitions of his creation, much like a craftsman's character and ideas are expressed in the work he does. God is not random, capricious, unpredictable or unknowable. He is not a magician, but the creator. He is not the arbitrary power capable of everything that people so often imagine as the cause of all the contradictions in life. God is in fact bound to himself first,[14] and then also by contracts or covenants which he made with creation and human beings.[15] He is invisible, but not hidden; holy and perfect, but not unapproachable. God is authority, but not an authoritarian dictator or boss. He explains life and its purpose, first to Adam and Eve[16] and then through prophets, apostles, and his Son to everyone else.

What God's word states must be true to the real world, must make sense to clear minds in order to be a reliable source of information. Such consistency between form and content can and must be shown. God chose to make a certain kind of world, he describes it accurately, and commits himself to it. It is his choice and thus forever binding. God

---

14. Consider the discussion in Jean Bethke Elshtain's *Sovereignty: Pope, State, Self* (Basic Books, 2008).

15. Noah, Abraham, the people Israel, and all believers of God are partners to such covenants of promise.

16. Gen 1:28–30.

cannot lie and yet remain God or good: he is bound to his own character and cannot act randomly and still be God.

God's definition for Man, male and female, is to be persons who think, act, and have emotions as well. Man, by his nature and by mandates from God, can and must choose: we reason, weigh alternatives, decide in matters of taste and intentions, and through our choices create new things, combinations, and relationships. We use language to communicate and ideas as well as our hands and bodies to rule over the earth,[17] to love our spouses, and to have children.[18] Men and women together are equally in the image of God and in charge of creation to discover and use it, harness its energies, and confidently labor in it for our increasing benefit and enjoyment.

Words, Grammar and Meaning

It is interesting that the Scriptures address Man in full sentences and well developed paragraphs rather than only in stories, parables, or images. The book develops God's ideas for us historically, with explanations that enter our minds to make us think, because we need to understand rather than mimic or recite and repeat. When this text speaks to us about moral character in real history we become aware that we need to discern, reflect, and evaluate. "Be fruitful and multiply"[19] makes one sit up and ponder what that implies, how to carry it out, what the command contains, and what further responsibilities we take up when we do just as we have been told.

Words addressed to our minds also point out the importance of wise discernment, as when we read, "Do not eat from the tree . . . or you will know (i.e. make the experience of) good and evil and will die."[20] We find here an order from God, the authority, an explanation to help us first understand and then embrace and own what should be done. The text alerts us to true human and historic significance.

---

17. Gen 1:26, 28.
18. Gen 2:24ff.
19. Gen 1:28.
20. Gen 2:16–17.

The Choice for Life and Against Death

In this connection we must notice that God did not want Adam and Eve to have the experience of both good and evil. He knew what that would be like but wanted people to be kept from what would be painful and destructive. God knew the difference, distinguished one from the other, and realized that human beings would not always be able to make that distinction if both good and evil were part of their normal daily experience.

God so valued Adam and Eve, the first human beings, that he put them into a well-prepared world, surrounded by good.[21] He planted a luscious garden rich with soil and plenty of water to make plants sprout abundantly as food for animals and human beings.[22] God took ample time for that, six periods of creativity before the world was ready for the persons he made in his image.[23]

Unlike animals, we have the benefits and obligations of trained minds and the responsibility to discern between choices. That is totally different from the mechanics of instinctual responses dominant in animal behavior.[24] Our minds possess intellectual and moral abilities that transcend the immediate moment, so that a distinct intimacy is possible with the persons of the Godhead. Paul, in speaking to philosophers in Athens, reiterates this filial reality between God and human beings with the words "in him (God) we live and move and have our being."[25]

In that capacity, our calling is to cultivate the earth, to work and keep it, not for selfish purposes, but using nature as God intended.[26] His own use of and admiration for the orderly functioning of creation should be the model we follow.[27]

As mentioned above, the time God took to prepare involved changes, additions, and innovations in a linear and sequential direction. There would be an eighth day following the seventh, then a ninth and all the

---

21. Gen 2:8. The Hebrew verb has the meaning of a pluperfect: a longer past before the more recent past.

22. Gen 2:8–15.

23. They are called "days" for the same reason we refer to a period of history, as in "the days of Rome." Evening and morning refer to the beginning and end of such periods.

24. Gen 2:2.

25. Acts 17:28, probably quoting Epimenides of Crete.

26. See Pierre Berthoud's insights in *En quête des origins* (Kerygma/Excelsis, 2010), 224ff.

27. Job 38:39ff.

days until now for both God and human beings in the same flow of history. Human activity includes constant efforts to diversify, review, add, grow, and since the fall of Adam and Eve, to resist evil and death.

Dominion Through Knowledge

Human beings are singled out as unique persons, wanted and loved by God. With that distinction come the special responsibilities contained in the phrase "have dominion." We are regents for God, which implies that an account will have to be given one day for the way we execute the task of being human and having dominion. As stewards for God on earth we are not autonomous; rather we are like late arrivals hired to work someone else's fields.[28]

Without the Bible's alternative propositions, many people read only a message of repetition in the "book of nature." The sun and moon seem to our eyes to go around the earth, the sea rises and falls regularly with the tides, and the seasons of the year, governed by increasing and decreasing exposure to the sun, repeat each other. In our experience people are born and then die. Security and belonging are found in conformity, where everyone follows tradition, and conforms. They count on repeatable patterns, on doing always the same.

Repetition creates a mentality of "again and again." It embraces the known and provides stability in knowing what comes next. It avoids fear of the unknown, but also denies the concept and then the possibility of improvement, of learning from mistakes, of a critical discernment at every stage of work, life, and development. While much of life becomes just "normal," this outlook also takes away the moral challenge and ability to discern and oppose wrong, whatever is irrational and contradictory to life, and finally death itself.

In fact, this outlook makes it that much more difficult to understand novel things and unusual events, which are consequently thought to be the work of evil spirits.

When God's text affects people's thoughts and directs their actions they have a different source for their security. It lies not in obedience to what seems normal, but in God's own reliable, stable, faithful character. In a fallen world we do not learn about God's character and intentions

---

28. Matt 25:14–30 gives us the parable of the talents, differently used and variably rewarded.

from what happens normally. The turn of events in an impersonal, uncaring, fallen, and indifferent nature should instead be seen from the critical distance that is always available to human beings who have a life of the mind that makes possible a vantage point above what is otherwise only random events.

The Bible gives us the tools we need to evaluate what God says. The mind registers through the senses *what already is; what ought to be* is not only imagined and hoped for in our mind, but also confirmed by what God's text tells us about his original work and intention. By means of that information God frees people for a dynamic, creative life, full of innovations and moral, factual, and cultural discernment. He made the world with specific forms "according to their kind," which thinking, caring, working minds and hands constantly affect each new day. Where we encounter the fallen world with its corrupted forms, we must also affect it through moral and practical resistance. We are commanded to be "imitators of God" in all domains.[29]

Life in an Open History

In the biblical understanding, the world is set on a developing path, where everything that was good from the beginning will constantly evolve, be multiplied and diversified through human imagination, action, and creativity under the rich blessing of God. New things will be discovered and produced as we subdue and make use of the original creation God placed under us.[30] Since the Fall of Adam, new forms of evil will also be invented at the same time, and must be fought in every domain, though they may become 'normal' in a broken world.

God had all that in mind when he mandated that humans should have dominion; Adam was to name the animals, and discover that each man and woman was totally unlike them. God was pleased and delighted when the first humans created their unique relationship and became one flesh, heart, and mind with the particular names of Adam and Eve; when they discovered and gave names to the animals, "which God would then also call them"[31]; and when they later had babies, in which God delighted for them. No day was meant to be a simple repetition of other days, no

---

29. Eph 5:1.
30. Gen 1:28.
31. Gen 2:19–20.

child a clone of either parent. Humans were given dominion to invent, create, and diversify, to be original in their unique personality and historic situation. God was pleased with each additional discovery and effort they made for good.

The Purpose of Being Human

The purpose of our being people, then, is to become fully human, bearing the image of God and creatively engaging in all that makes life possible. God wants us to be people, not stones, sticks, or animals. Our pattern "according to our kind" is discernment and choice, not repetition or resignation. We face tomorrow with the knowledge of today and the desire to learn and do more, to make it a unique and possibly outstanding day.

That is well expressed in Psalm 8. There we that God made us "a little lower than the angels,"[32] with mandates to work, multiply, control our choices and lives, and love and discipline ourselves as responsible creatures.[33] We should reflect and decide, and explain the reasons for our choices to ourselves, our neighbor, and God. Following that pattern of being human is the central way in which we believe God, love him, and enjoy him forever.

How different human beings are from everything else! On the level of our bodies we are related to the earth in its diverse forms, taking food and drink from it. On the level of our mind, spirit, and soul we are related to God and our neighbors around the world. We are made in God's image and he teaches us. From him we receive the ideas that inform us about what it is to be human, moral, and responsible. We learn from nature about our bodies, but from God and our neighbors about our minds, meaning, and morality.

You remember that animals function largely from instincts or a biological pattern that defines them. A few additional patterns can be taught to an animal, but they do not choose or have a say in whether their skin or fur is warm or cold, where they will live, whether they walk, swim, or fly, nor how or what they express with the sounds they make. Cats and squirrels will land on their feet. Animals mate to reproduce and plants are fertilized to bear flowers or fruit.

---

32. Ps 8:5–9.
33. This is exactly what Genesis already states in 1:26 and 2:17.

People, however, are able to think, feel, and act, because God thinks, feels, acts and tells us about it. We learn from increasing knowledge, by instruction, and with motivation. We choose our clothes, where and how to live and work, make love and communicate with words to tell the truth as well as to joke and deceive. We must learn discernment and depend on explanations, texts, and discussion, weighing wisdom against foolishness.

Most of the time we do not naturally, "in our nature," know what to do. We need instruction and encouragement, memory and an inquisitive mind. But even then we need to question the source, application, and practical usefulness of any instructions in order to avoid mistakes among many available options. We need to look around with curiosity, apply a healthy amount of critical evaluation, and inquire more from experts than elders. Knowledge and wisdom come neither at birth nor with age, but from research and critical thinking.

We must ask and learn, daring to explore alternatives about what to do, make, and sell, how to raise children and love our spouses, and how to organize life with neighbors of all kinds. For that reason the God of the Bible promises to give us far more than commands or directives. He promises insightful ideas and sensitive discernment because we do not naturally find them in our mind and heart, or even in our community.

One more observation: food from field and forest is provided by the way God created nature, but must be prepared by human hands to meet man's physical needs. Knowledge is given to our minds to satisfy our spiritual and intellectual need. It warns against such enormous dangers as confusing love with sexual violence and exploitation, replacing affection with indifference, or turning from action to resignation. Truth is a filter against the exercise of power and violence over those who, without it, have given up on taking a stand. Now they often just follow, stupidly.

A person will make his or her own decisions in work and love, in ethics and aesthetics. God or nature do not tell us whether we should live in cities, arid lands, or forests, whether we should work in factories or in the field. We can change language groups and nations. What cannot be changed is that to be really "at home," and therefore safe and comfortable in our decisions, we require outside information about how to be purposeful, moral human beings. We look around for models and instruction, but without the personal God of the Bible we have only two functioning models available: one is impersonal nature, from the smallest virus to the largest beast, each a humiliating, intellectually silent, indifferent, and often cruel master. The second is the clan, group, or society, which either functions by a morally variable consensus or by imposed invariable patterns.

Human beings are very complicated but also unique in the ability to use our minds rather than our few and mostly underdeveloped instincts.[34] Our choices are not programmed, and our minds will readily justify both good and evil ones. We can create problems but we can also choose to become agents who work toward solutions in line with what God intended for us to do. That is, indeed, our calling, like a directive from the creator: to be human beings in his image, to work in his creation, to create life, and to benefit from the riches God makes possible for thinking, working, and loving people in their interplay with the natural riches of raw materials in creation. People can transform natural things into tools for a "good life."

In the next section we will see how God's work reveals the specific characteristics of his personality and the manner of his governance that illustrate how we should care for our work, employees, and community. We are responsible to provide instruction to other people so that they will benefit from their abilities and desires.

---

34. Ps 139:14: "I am fearfully (Hebrew: 'set apart') and wonderfully made."

Chapter 6

Good Model for Governance

THE PRECEDING CHAPTER EXPLORED how well God governs his creation, how thoughtfully he put it together, and how he ennobles people to be his regents on earth. The early chapters of Genesis lay the groundwork for understanding the world we live in and describe the wonderful governance of God over his creation. That stands in stark contrast to what people often do with their lives. We need to return to the example of God's governance in order to find a model and an outlook to repair our damaged situation and help restore healthy human relationships.

The contemporary crisis of governance in many areas, including families, businesses, and whole countries (and not only those in the process of development), should challenge us to study how the Bible illustrates the Creator's principles. We can then address the crisis of management in our own lives, our family relations, business practices, social interactions, and political efforts.

People are increasingly disrespectful to each other in social contexts, whether as husbands and wives, parents and children, or employers and employees. Essentially human relationships have become battlegrounds. There is little peace in the "polis" of a city, community, company, or state when the dominant goal is to win or rule rather than to pursue what is good and wise for the benefit of every social and economic relationship.

We can begin to address and resolve existing problems by first recognizing where real friction and disruption occur. It is of course far easier to just let history or market forces take care of problems and wait to see how things develop rather than do the hard work of looking for a solution. This is especially so when diverse and painful human relations are presented as cultural alternatives that we should simply accept. When all reasonable moral considerations are obliterated, all complaints cease to have a justification and no improvement is possible. That view creates an attitude of non-interference in the suffering of others and denies them their share in our common human dignity.

Christians must set out to do more than repeat old patterns because we are mandated to show kindness and comprehension, to feel deep sorrow over the shards which we create by smashing what God made well and good. To do this we must improve our hitherto insufficient understanding of the teaching of the Scriptures, both in its express statements and in its vivid illustrations of the way God acts in relation to what he decided to make and continues to treasure. The God of the Bible and the person of Jesus do not agree with everything that happens through human hands and from human minds, or from tragic natural fractures in history.

The largely neglected biblical concept of creation by God needs to be rediscovered for its broader practical and philosophical benefits. That may come as a surprise. Most believers affirm creation, of course, but only in quite a limited way. They are mostly interested in questions concerning the age of the earth and perhaps the possibility and degree of developmental change over time, due to the interplay, the push, shove, and rub between all created things.

But the concept of an original creation promotes a wider philosophical interest, because we discover there something of the intentions in God's acts. Living with and in a created world tells us far more about God's approach and decisions, and consequently what ours should be every day.

God's Beneficial Governance

The Bible lists the acts of God at the beginning of the creation of the universe in some detail and in sequence. However, when we read the Bible as a doctrinal/religious text rather than a text about procedures, intentions, and facts, we often, to our great loss, neglect the manner in which God went about creating. For *how* God creates in the first chapters of Genesis, with his pleasure and intentions, should encourage and influence us, who are made in his image, to understand our own responsibilities. We are all in places of authority, whether over others or only over ourselves, our thoughts, and choices. We should reflect on the wise and moral exercise of such authority.

God and Man at Work

In the first chapters of Genesis God is presented as a providential leader. That term needs an explanation. God's providence is not only what he approves with determination and agreement. God is not behind all events, a Greek Fate, Aristotle's "unmoved mover," or any other puppet master, pulling all the strings in an inevitable course of events in history.[1]

My use of the term "God's providence" refers rather to his own faithfulness, commitment, and passion to see things through to their purposed and envisioned end, even when it takes extra effort and much time to get things done, and real battles against evil and death to correct and repair what results of the derived authority of his creatures.

God's providential leadership means that from the start he provides in abundance for the needs of what he directs. In the original creation all things were made to function steadily according to their kind. God gives to Adam and Eve, though in a limited way because of their finiteness, the responsibilities to be like him as providential leaders. How is that apparent to us when we read the Bible?

Three Examples of Good Governance

God's providential governance is shown right at the beginning of the Bible in three distinct social/economic settings. The first two chapters of Genesis form a unit, followed by Genesis 3, which describes the interruption brought about by the introduction of sin in the world, and finally, Genesis 4 tells of the relationship between God and Cain.

These chapters describe God's continuing care for his creation in radically changing circumstances. The whole Bible continues that account and assumes familiarity with it. Though everything has changed because of sin, God's response is not principally marked by anger, frustration, and abandonment. Instead, what is evident is his gracious concern, deep compassion, and a desire to pursue his intentions in spite of obstacles now in the way which make a solution much harder to find and provide.

That effort carries forward what is part of God's character from the start. Already in Genesis 1 and 2 the providential governance of God the Creator is presented by at least six characteristic features or qualities.

First, God is benevolent and generous; he is of good will, not anxious, lacking imagination, or filled with fear. Out of the chaos of originally

---

1. Consider the arguments for such a view of providence in Udo Middelmann's *The Innocence of God* (Paternoster, 2007).

undifferentiated matter he creates a vibrant order that is diverse, bountiful, and increasingly defined, set to always grow and diversify. Through his many acts over time the undefined becomes a purposefully created diversity that functions well.

Second, God is a worker. His ideas are expressed in thought, word, and action, with skill and determination; he brings about a whole expanding, dynamic, and colorful universe. He thinks definitions and then speaks them into being as new, well-defined objects.

Third, God remains accessible and intimately available for those whom he directs. He walks in the garden he made, conversing with Adam and at all times taking delight in what he sees. It is a scene of mutual love and enjoyment.

Fourth, as Lord and director of creation he does not simply give orders, but creates a setting in which everything he made, whether plants, animals, or people, can flourish on its own level. He relates to people made in his image in a spirit that cultivates reflection and understanding.

Fifth, God entrusts a mandate for creative development to humans. They are not bound to a formula or a cycle of repetition. People are free to choose, new forms and characteristics which are intended to vary in the endless passing of time.

Last, God placed the reality of relationships, forms of connectedness, into creation, whether through chemical and physical forms of interactive processes between things, or through language, learning, and love between people. This gives privilege to the reality of working in teams, of collaboration instead of conflict and exploitation.

Many readers admire the account in Genesis where they come face to face with the scope and details of God's handiwork. He made the earth as a rich and abundant place to nourish and develop what thrives on it. Both Christian and Jewish biblical commentators remark on God's benevolence. They point out that the generosity of God, as evidenced in his work, is cause for appreciation when we recognize how humanity profits from it.

Many have compared the Creator with enthusiastic parents who await their first child. They ensure that all is ready to receive the child who will be born: a cradle is installed, the baby's garments are prepared, and everything is done so that the awaited child will receive the best possible reception. In particular, this generosity is apparent in how Adam and Eve are valued and treasured by God.

During the six distinct periods of creation, however long we think them to have been, God works with deliberate method and steady assiduity.

There is purpose and determination in the process. He does not stop in the middle of the project; it is carried out until the original goal is achieved. Then God rests, not from fatigue but for enjoyment. God evaluates his work and takes stock of what he has achieved. At the end of the sixth day he notices the loneliness of Adam and therefore goes back to work to correct this gap, creating a help meet for Adam but distinct from him.

This work of God is not limited to his divine calling to create. Before placing Adam in the garden he also engages in the needed work of agriculture: "The Lord God planted a garden in Eden with trees of every species, pleasant to see and good to be eaten."[2] God worked the ground he himself created. He planted trees not only for their own sake, but also to provide Adam and Eve with healthy food and a pleasant framework of life. By this alteration and transformation of the soil through the vocation of a farmer God shows the importance and value of manual work.

Instructions for Discerning Minds

God's engagement with his creation and with people does not stop with his preparations. He does not withdraw from the scene to leave Adam alone but remains close to him. He meets with Adam, not in the heavens, the residence of God, but on earth. We learn about the God of creation as a commuting God who displaces himself for proximity to Man. He knows the human need for such personal company, not only with God himself in order to understand the purpose of creation, but also with a thinking, loving, and touching person on Adam's own level of "creatureliness." That need could neither be filled by the benevolent presence of God, who is Spirit and not material, nor by that of the animals, which are material, but without a soul, language, or love. God meets this need, which he recognizes and understands, by the creation of Eve from Adam. Herein lies the foundation of the one human race on earth, prior to and more substantive than any subsequent developments in external appearance.

God communicates with Adam and Eve through language to explain the direction and purpose of creation so they can start to understand the place they must occupy. "Live, be fertile and eat from any plant carrying seed . . . and any tree bearing fruit."[3] God also alerts them about

---

2. Gen 2:8, 9.
3. Gen 1:29.

a dreadful danger: "You will not eat from the tree of the knowledge of the good and evil, because the day you eat of it, you will die."[4]

The words God speaks to Adam and Eve contain much more than mere information, advice, and warnings. With his work of creation as an example, God engages Adam and Eve in their own creative projects: they are called to procreate and to make the ground bear fruit. The instruction to "work and take care of the ground"[5] invites Adam and Eve to imagine a future different from their immediate present situation. It encourages them to understand that the world God entrusts to them is in the process of constant change, a world of development, where all that is already very good can evolve, diversify, multiply, and develop by the intellectual and physical work of man and woman under the blessing of God.

This changing creation is illustrated when God leads the animals to Adam in the garden to see what and how he will call them; thus God engages Man in the exploration and progressive discovery of the world. Adam did not need to name the animals in order to survive. The trees and the plants already provided him with food. However, his vocation from God goes beyond his immediate needs. By giving the animals their names, Adam fulfills the vocation of observation, proper scientific exploration, and classification.

The Significance of a Tri-One Godhead

Scripture describes creation as the result of the work of a personal God who thinks, feels, loves, and acts. These would be empty words, were the Bible not to point out a Trinity of three persons in a relationship of sequential give and take. They are able to be persons to one another forever in their divine plurality, while a single person would be forever alone, unable to love until a creature was made. The Trinity is the Bible's answer to two questions: why is there both unity and diversity and why do universals and particulars exist everywhere in the universe?

In the Scriptures the title of God is generally allotted to the Father, but he does not act alone. The Spirit already hovers above everything before God even pronounces his first creative words.[6] The apostle John

---

4. Gen 2:17.
5. Gen 2:15.
6. Gen 1:2.

affirms that it is by the Son that all was created.[7] Each of them played their part. Together and with love for one another they must have deliberated and decided *what* and *when* to create *which* heavens and earth.

In this Trinitarian Godhead the attentive reader discovers "the former," the model, the eternal foundation for our working together as distinct individuals in a family first and then, with a lesser bond, in society. God calls Adam and Eve together to develop his work as a team. For Adam, the discovery of Eve and then the idea to engage in the work of long development with her who is "bone of my bones and flesh of my flesh" is very good news. The advantage of a division of labor for mutual benefit through teamwork is obvious on any project.

God in Search of People

More evidence of the providential direction of God in creation comes after the fall in Genesis 3. In spite of Adam and Eve's rebellion and the terrible fracture their sin produced in the goodness of the original creation and the harm, pain, and death that followed, God continues to lead them, remaining at all times benevolent and generous. His interest and desire guide the way he continuously surrounds his creatures. Rather than turning his back on them he protects them and all creation against their attitudes and destructive behavior.

Following their disobedience, when Adam and Eve experience the consequences of their choice, God does not inflict a "maximum punishment" on them. The effect of the fall destroys neither their person nor their habitat. While respecting his own law, God does not make Adam and Eve pay the complete price of their fault. God is the compassionate one, whose generosity makes up their defects as he requires that price of himself. The generous mercy of God demonstrates clearly how much he continues to value Adam and Eve in spite of their condemnable actions. He does not cut off his investment in creating people in the first place. Instead, he renews it with the temporary "forsaking" of his Son.[8]

God continuously surrounds and protects them and all creation with his care and provisions.

Adam and Eve's rebellion bring about important damages in their relation with God, their own lives, and creation. Culprits now, they flee

7. John 1:3.
8. Matt 27:46.

God, attempting to hide from him. However, God does not abandon them where they hide, but seeks them out in order to meet them face to face. In the manner of a human magistrate, God could have dispatched angels to transport Adam and Eve, *manu militari*, in front of a celestial court. Or he could have turned his back on them when they chose to be bad. But he did neither. Like a good shepherd, an image well known in the agrarian setting of simple societies,[9] he goes as far as necessary to find them, even if from shame they do not wish to encounter him.

God's Investment in People

Then and there God commits himself for the long run and sets out to repair his damaged creation. He promises a final victory over the destroyer, over evil and death, even though they continue to do everything to prevent the lasting development of creation.

God is also engaged in the short term, the immediate context. In spite of sin's corruption of the world, God does not distance himself from it. He clothes Adam and Eve from the skin of an innocent animal he kills in their stead, which becomes their first experience of death as a substitute for what they deserved. The later sacrifice of an animal throughout Jewish history, until it became impossible with the destruction of the temple in Jerusalem in 70 AD, was not a way to please, appease, or manipulate God with something a person gave up. Instead it served as a daily reminder of God's provision to cover the damage Adam and Eve had caused and then passed to all mankind.[10]

Jewish sacrifices are a constant reminder of both the tragedy of life in a fallen world and of the hope that we will be taken care of by a loving and providing God.

When God finds Adam and Eve, he confronts them with the disastrous consequences of their disobedience. Yet he does not simply give that information to them. Instead, he engages them in a conversation by raising questions. God does not lack the answer but wants to restore broken communication with them and lead them to reflect on their new condition and their continuing, permanent vocation as human beings.

God does not cancel Adam and Eve's responsibilities in the world, in spite of their irresponsible behavior. Even though the curse weighs

---

9. Jesus uses the same image in the parable of the lost sheep in Luke 15.
10. Rom 5:12ff.

on everything in history because of their sin, God does not withdraw his earlier mandate to develop the ground as well as themselves. This responsibility is later confirmed to the next generation and again after the flood, when God communicates hope to the human race,[11] and promises never to give up on his created world that was made to be developed and habitable.[12] He pledges to overcome even the source of destruction, the devil and all he intended, provoked, and caused.

There is more in these passages to observe and appreciate. God also does not cease collaborating with those who rebel against him. By his presence and his promises he indicates his intention to continue working with people. God does not definitively reject bad collaborators. He does not eliminate them. Quite the contrary, he invites them to take up their functions again, even while taking on the burden of the consequences of their acts. It is important to notice that even though Adam and Eve are now inclined to accuse each other, to shrug their shoulders, and to hide from each other, God does not cancel their marriage. He confirms their responsibility to act as a team[13] and sends them together out of Eden and into the world.

Furthermore, God as a provident director in the Book of Genesis also exhibits benevolence towards Cain in the next generation. Initially, God clearly says that the refusal of Cain's offering is not a rejection of him as a person. For God invited him to overcome his failure by presenting an excellent and acceptable offering like that of his brother. God takes the trouble to warn Cain against the destructive nature of jealousy.

Mercy is also present when God does not remove Cain even after the murder of his younger brother. Even then God shows mercy by protecting him against those who want to kill him to avenge Abel's death. God exerts what one could describe as "tough love." He punishes the crime but does not destroy the criminal, even protecting him from revenge by others.

God remains accessible and available. He does not give up on Cain, but meets and speaks with him. Before the crime God informs and instructs him. After the murder, God inflicts its punishment on Cain and excludes him from his family of origin but does not remove his vocation to work, live, and develop a genuine life.

---

11. Gen 9:11.
12. Isa 45:18.
13. Gen 3:16.

Good Model for Governance

To that end God cultivates a spirit of comprehension and understanding in Cain, both before and after his crime. God comes to him in the same way he approached his parents when they disobeyed in the garden. God questions Cain in order to give him the opportunity to reflect on himself and his situation. Then God gives him hope for his vocation and future development as a person who would continue to live in the world.

When Cain is excluded from his clan because of his sin, God offers him protection and hope in spite of this punishment. On a distant soil far away, abroad, one could say, he and his descendants live out their mandate to develop the world, to make it subject, and to have dominion over it. Cain founds a large family, is productive, and builds the first city mentioned in the history of the world.[14] His children also do not lack creativity, for one invents musical instruments, and another creates and refines work tools.[15]

We can all be comforted and reassured that God does not give up collaborating with those who disobey him. A person is valuable and loved already as a person per se, not only when he or she obeys. Although Cain distances himself from God after his crime, God does not deprive him of his human vocation to be a creative, enterprising person. God protects him and offers him the possibility of procreating and contributing through children to the building of a diverse human community to further the development of the world and its resources.

Think of how your life and that of your community and business could benefit from applying the principles behind God's actions and attitudes to each area of your responsibilities. To help, let us sum up what we have learned.

The first chapters of Genesis introduce the person of God who, in the exercise of his authority, explains a purposeful reality created with deliberation and much pleasure for himself and for people. From the beginning he models certain attitudes and practices we should understand and emulate in our own circles of private, public, and business life.

Rather than aloof, authoritarian, or disinterested in details, God in his Being is generous and full of passion, delight, and mercy. He is busily at work rather than being an absent master who scorns manual work.[16]

---

14. Gen 4:17.

15. Gen 4:21ff.

16. One can observe that in better restaurants the owner and the maitre d' work alongside the waiters. We all work better when we are side-by-side with the boss, and when he or she also pitches in. I recall a builder on an African construction site who

He is present at all times and has his eye on each participant. God takes the first step to approach people where they are, even in uncomfortable and adverse circumstances. God takes the initiative of going to his people in order to inform them, encourage and correct them, to make promises, and to offer ways for reconciliation. At times he uses directives, at other times he awakens greater awareness and responsibility by asking questions in order to make those whom he directs reflect on the causes and significance of their present situation.

Similarly, God administers justice and judgment, though rarely through active intervention. Rather judgment usually occurs in the form of painful and obvious consequences to prior actions. But even in punishment God never destroys our fundamental vocation as humans. We can continue to develop ourselves and the world by creative imagination and personal engagement, by learning from error and changing the direction of our lives. God favors and supports human collaboration, mutual dependence, and team interaction for the creation of profitable communities in the development of the world.

Jesus Christ and the apostle Paul exhibited the same qualities of leadership. Today, families, businesses, and all the countries of the world, whether developed or along the way, need leaders who adopt and follow these concerns, and who understand, seek, and develop these same qualities for the practice of good governance. A good boss, chief, father, or mother is one who recognizes and conforms to what works in the real world, a world God made in a certain way and continues to manage faithfully, true to his character. For that reason we are told to have the mind of Christ,[17] to be like God, to understand his word, and do justice[18] to it and to all creation.

This has nothing to do with Satan's false promise, "You will be like god." It is rather the invitation to be a good master, boss, entrepreneur, employer, and parent out of respect for the supreme model of God as director and worker, whose rational character is exposed to us in the workings of creation. In response to what God has told us we must choose our responsibilities and continue to reflect the careful providence which he executes around us.

---

kept his workers busy and committed with fewer interruptions when he left his glass eye on a table during his infrequent but at times necessary absences. He was able to keep "an eye" on things!

17. Phil 2:5.
18. John 10:34ff.

In the next section we will discover why so many problems exist in spite of the good model and advice we receive from the Bible. We do not exclusively experience a beautiful world; in its present state we have, with wonderful exceptions, little security among our neighbors and in nature around us. Reality includes many dangers. For most people life is often painful, unfair, and easily threatened. It is abnormal compared to what the Bible presents and what we long for when we expect things to go the way they should.

Chapter 7

Tragic Elements of Life

Everyone acknowledges that there are real problems in the world. These are not simply engineering problems or the results of ignorance, both of which could be fixed with more energy and tools or an education. People do not hurt only themselves, they also make choices which bring hardship, pain, and often death, deliberately or not, into the lives of others. In addition there are incapable, often corrupt governments and nasty neighbors, broken families and other hurtful institutions, even churches. There is no end to things going wrong and much of human effort is a pain that ends in frustration.

Even those who assume that everything is normal or happens by necessity still complain about pain, wrong, and in the end death. Everyone eventually calls for help in some form or other. The realization that something is not right forcefully confronts us in the contrast between the great effort we put into living, from birth as a fragile human baby to our continuing efforts to stay healthy, alive, and secure, and the reality of an unstable life, untimely aging, and death. In fact, the dust of death, the exposure to death, is with us at all times. Death is the most certain thing, coming to everyone equally, independent of status, wealth, gender, religion, geography, moral behavior, or even age.

When I speak of death with all its ugly faces I mean more than the termination of physical existence. Long before that occurs there is already death in the form of broken and therefore 'dead' relationships, unsafe environments, or insufficient protection where laws do not provide definite and equal punishment for all transgressors. I see death in the action of hostile nature and in the uncomfortable and humiliating decline of intellectual and physical abilities with increasing age. Finally, I also refer to

Tragic Elements of Life

death in the narrower sense. Survivors are left only with someone's body, and then only for a little while until it decomposes. That body is not the person we knew, and yet we did not know a person without a body. In any case, someone must dispose of a corpse.

How does the presence of death in all its ugly forms relate to God's assertion that he is the good creator of a good and beautiful creation? Does any possibility remain for belief in such a God? Each generation forever raises this question. Failing to satisfy it has led many people to conclude that there is no God worth speaking about. And neither should they, if God is indeed the author of the world we know and in control of it with all its problems. As the French poet Charles Baudelaire[1] is reputedly said, if God created this world, he must be the devil.

Until a few decades ago most people in every culture believed that death is a painful and regrettable interruption of life. They set out to make provisions for a continuing life after death by placing food, clothes, armor, and sometimes even young wives or virgins into the grave for a future existence. But recent generations in the West have begun to look at death as just another phase of life. They have adopted what was unthinkable in a pagan and a Biblical outlook about death's rupture of life. In fact they replace what the Bible indicates about the abnormality of death as an enemy to be fought at every stage with the acceptance that it is normal. They close up life and death in a cyclical sequence and abandon the linear view of history that includes the hope of an historic resurrection of the whole person, body, soul, and spirit on earth. Seeking so-called "closure," they deny the contrast between life and death and make God, if he is still referred to at all, the author of a life that includes death, and actively embrace it instead of opposing it.

If death is part of the will of God then life has always involved death from the beginning, and consequently life and death are equally part of the normal, originally intended sequence. A painful reaction to these "opposites" reveals a mistaken response to what is really all the same show. Death is just the last in a series of events called life.

Moral neutrality is increasingly demanded where this view is widely held. Death is no longer the enemy to be fought with skill, medical intervention, and physical force; nature, history, and science relate only to a cycle of life in which all moral discernment is just the vestige of an older, emotional view.

---

1. April 9, 1821–August 31, 1867.

We see in this change a renewed embrace of Greek philosophical thought. Death becomes a form of deliverance into a better condition in which the person is freed from the burden of a physical body connected to time.

The Bible stands out with a rejection of these interpretations. The reality of death is acknowledged. Of course, even those who think death a dream, an illusion, or normal, behave rather abnormally with their tears and sorrow. And regardless of what they believe they have a real body to dispose of! Death's abnormality is always expressed in words, signs, and rituals. No one is really able to see death as merely a statistic on a timeline. Ceremonies always express some regret, pain, even anger—all unjustified if everything is only natural and necessary.

Opposing Death With All One's Life

Contradictions of this kind are not required or encountered in the Bible which considers death to be a late arrival on the scene of human life. It had no part in the original creation. Death cannot be made beautiful; it is a tragedy, a horror, to be fought, opposed, and repelled. It will not remain forever nor become normal. Death will be the last enemy to be conquered[2] and destroyed by the same power that raised Jesus to real material life as the first fruit of a fuller harvest of resurrected people who will never die.

If you believe there is no contradiction between life and death, there is nevertheless a tension that surfaces at every funeral. Different attempts have been made to resolve this tension. Three major propositions are mentioned here.

You may conclude that you deserve death, that you are a waste of space, hopelessly worthless, or needing punishment. People in the jungle of Gabon believe the earth was not made for human habitation and that everything is geared to destroy them. Wild animals, malaria, and evil spirits in the dark forest all bring about death to human beings.

In a second attempt, you may conclude that nature (or God) is good, so the problem is all in your faulty mind. You must then adjust your perception in order not to be upset by death. Your way of thinking must be adapted, for wrong is only an interpretation in your analytical mind. It does not really exist in an external, objective reality. Moral and

2. 1 Cor 15:26.

factual analysis must be replaced by non-judging synthetic approach, which calls for detachment in order to see everything as part of a great Oneness, participating in a uniting flow over time. Through synthesis all tensions are removed, a both/and perspective replaces the either/or. Until now you analyzed events and thought something was really wrong in the world. However, when you no longer see opposites, the wrong disappears and you can call everything good or bad, or whatever, bowing to the all-encompassing One.[3]

Last, you may conclude that there is in fact something truly ugly justifying your agony and protest, something really wrong with the natural world or with God, who made it in the first place! You are left with either the work of an indifferent nature or an evil, capricious, or incapable divinity.

We can sum up the three options like this: either bad things happen because we are useless misfits, without honor or worth; or there is something wrong with the way we see and interpret things as bad, painful, and objectionable; or our perception is correct and the wrong has always been there.

In all three cases, our pain and sorrow are evidence that we apply moral discernment *before* we accept a proposed solution. People truly experience pain and suffering, often without a sufficient explanation for it or deliverance from it. The impersonal universe cannot assuage our grief.

Behind each consideration lies the assumption that everything has always been the same, with no fundamental change in the continuous functioning of reality. We correctly assume this in science, which operates on the basis of continuity in all physical things. Science is so helpful when it lets us draw conclusions from past observations. The regularity confirms laws, making predictions about likely future outcomes sensible. Science can make valid statements because we do not live in a world of constant change. A new day begins with some certainty gained from past observations.

It is a reasonable assumption that what is now must have always been, and is therefore normal and not out of line. With no interference or change between causes and their effects, reality is in a steady state and has always been this way.

All the religions I know join together in a common conclusion based on that observation. The words may differ and the prescribed

---

3. We discussed this alternative in chapter 1.

practices vary. But that only superficially hides that there are few philosophic variables among all religions. They all teach that the big problems of pain, death, evil, and injustice exist only in the human mind's ability to imagine an alternative, which must therefore be suppressed. Problems are resolved when you stop thinking so seriously about them, accept what is there, and understand that there is nothing else to do. Common to all religions, including Marxism, is the requirement that you distance yourself from the weight of your own moral feelings and perceived pain[4]. Comfort is offered in religious practices and repeated phrases, ideological instruction, fanatical repetition and a shrug of the shoulders, and an appeal to destiny. They all support the status quo as inevitable and therefore "normal."

Religions detach people from their genuine and intimate selves in the real world and join them to an interpretation, a belief, a community. But the question remains: is there nothing else that would acknowledge real pain and loss in the face of death, as well as justify well-founded hope in a good God?

Going on Without God

Many conclude that if there is any God at all, he is either absent, weak, or wicked. This view is accepted widely today among modern people who arrive at this perspective for several reasons.

First, much of reality can be explained by a reasonable and detailed knowledge of how things work. Observation leads to scientific laws based on regular patterns and repeatable experiments. From these findings we can extrapolate future activity with reasonable confidence. This ability to sufficiently understand and manage life makes the belief in God as creator and sustainer largely unnecessary for many people. Increasing knowledge about why things happen and how to improve them has replaced the former reference to God as the reason for drought, sickness, or any kind of damage. Finding many cures for real problems seems to demonstrate that God is not the power behind events, so one can manage quite well without belief in him. The *deus ex machina*, the God of the stopgap who suddenly appears in the conversation when no reasonable answer remains, is less

---

4. A Buddhist saying tells us that "pain is real, but suffering is an option." It hints that your experience of pain can be avoided by mental choice. A Christian view instead proposes using the mind to find ways to eliminate the causes of real pain in the external world.

and less called upon. The physical and chemical components of the real world function in an interrelated manner; nothing truly new is caused, and the god-option or explanation is no longer needed.

Many reasonable, verifiable explanations of things and events show that belief in God as the immediate power behind everything was wrong, a case of hiding a culture of ignorance under the bright cloth of assumed spirituality. But that is unnecessary if Christians properly understand that all things in God's creation function "according to their kind," through time and space, along a path determined by what they were created to be. There is no act of God in the growth of apples on an apple tree, for God made it to function as an apple tree. There is no act of God in the creation of a human baby, for God made men and women to have babies as part of the way they function. Conception is a recurring fact in a reasonable universe, not a specific act of God.

Without God Only Gaping Ignorance

Yet the denial of God's real existence leaves two central questions without sufficient answers. First, in contrast to a random or chaotic universe, why is our universe one of order and form, in which general and specific laws about the way things function can be established?[5] The Bible anchors our observation of order in the proposition that God created things "according to their kind" and that he was "well pleased" with them. Order is displayed in both the grammar of human language and the sense of moral distinctions. A chaotic universe would have neither grammar nor moral reasoning.

The other unanswered question for the secularist concerns the origin of the human person: how can personality with real freedom of choice and the consequent responsibilities, with a mental life of imagination and language, proceed from the closed system of impersonal, chemical, and physical forces? How can thought occur out of matter, freedom from form, and the unnecessary from necessary links? How can the human person (a "fact") deliberately tell lies, make jokes, invent and distribute propaganda, and declare and deceive one's love?

A second reason to deny God or to see him as weak or wicked is that reality gives evidence of permanent flaws, whether personal pain,

---

5. The universe we inhabit is one-of-a-kind and therefore incomparable to anything else.

sickness and death, bad government, poor soil or climate, or natural disasters quite generally. Many today conclude that because of the pain in the real world there could not be any God. For them the world is in constant flux from one stage of development to another; pain and death are real, but only part of the normal tensions in the push and shove of energy and tectonic movements. Because of survival instincts, these people will work to diminish personal pain and enjoy life a little more.

Religions are then understood to merely offer remedies to those who need them. They function on the same order as drugs and at times even wars against neighboring countries: they avoid exposure to real problems and the need to address them through the reasoned exploration of alternatives.

The two unanswered problems remain. First, if we suppose that the way things are is normal, then there is nothing to complain about. It is a meaningless tautology to say that the universe functions the way it functions or that the fit survive. Then why are we dissatisfied, or if we are, why should it matter to anyone beyond a statistical note? Why don't we accept things as they are, as impersonal stones do their place in nature?

Second, what or who validates our moral standards by which we judge things to be unacceptable? A complaint has significance and we are justified in seeking a culprit only if something could have been avoided because it was *not* inevitable.

Such unresolved questions and problems set up an opposition between religions that deny the human being as a thinking, critical, personal being, and secularism, which denies any lasting and reliable standard for moral discernment based on God. Neither proposition satisfies the challenges arising out of our human existence.

The Good News About Adam's Fall

Picture the scene in a court room in which the Bible and its God stand accused but ready to lay out a defense we need to consider. The argument for the defense is that it is the only alternative to the common belief in the normality of everything. Rather than seeing a continuing natural world in a straight line, the Bible claims that something terrible occurred after creation. We are familiar with other forms of catastrophic events or choices, which stain everything now differently and make reality "abnormal" in comparison to what existed before, when everything was the way it was intended. A new situation comes about, in nature because of earthquakes or tidal waves, and in history as the consequence of deliberate human action. Instead of a steady state universe, the Bible proposes a catastrophic view of history: a catastrophe broke into what once was natural and lawful.

The flow of time has been jolted. There has been a bang and a leap from what was whole to what is now cracked. Rather than natural and lawful events in an uninterrupted chain of cause and effect, there has been interference through the choice of significant creatures. History is full of the effects of human choice, from greatness to naked evil, from the irresponsible exploitation of natural resources to the clever invention of the internal combustion engine that harnesses an explosion to turn wheels.

According to the Bible, God has not changed and is still good. All things are still regular and lawful, but marked by the profound effect of a human creative choice that changed the course of history, making life now abnormal, painful, and in the end fatal. The world and everything in it is no longer how God created it. It is a damaged world of imperfect and sinful people, with nature wounded and things falling apart.

We should not approve the condition of this world or accept it as final. Rather, we can find great comfort knowing that it was not this way originally and that it will not be this way forever.

In the view put forth in the Bible today's reality is not inevitable; it did not need to happen in this way. It was not intended by God. In contrast to what was originally designed and made, the world is now damaged, dangerous, and often painful. In their present state, then, creation, nature, and history do not reveal God's character or purposes. We still see God's eternal power and divine nature[6] in creation, but not his character, holiness, or intentions. We learn of these and other attributes only in a text from God and his prophets that tells us things, for instance the commandments,[7] not clearly visible in what was made. The text, the Bible, gives a direction for thought and practice that differs from what nature, including human nature, would readily suggest. According to the Bible the exact image of God the Father is Jesus,[8] not nature or history.

---

6. Rom 1:20.
7. Deut 8:3 and Matt 4:4.
8. Heb 1:1–4.

God and Man at Work

History Always Accused

This understanding allows us to see history neither as the exclusive work of God, nor something that always pleases God. We are not obligated to approve of all its twists and turns or blindly bow to its actors. Instead we must critique it in thought and deed from the outside perspective of moral criteria presented in the Bible and in the person and life of Jesus Christ. We should continuously complain about what is wrong[9] and set out to diminish the damage and repair the broken bits.[10] Life is no longer what it was created to be. Most dramatically, death is a latecomer, an enemy to be fought, resisted, and given no respect.[11]

The Bible's propositions are unique in their rational and moral clarity. They are the intellectual foundation for the Enlightenment concern for truth, when authoritarian pronouncements of Church and State were questioned and often rightly rejected in light of more detailed knowledge of facts on the ground and greater awareness that the claims of those in authority were often irrational.

I know of no other outlook which so honors human beings and is in agreement with the Biblical perspective from which it is derived. Its singular approach to life is the reason people enlightened by its teaching struggle for more than subsistence and survival, and reject "waiting for the end" or "going to heaven" as a way out. Moral clarity and practical efforts result from the biblical understanding that creation is damaged and needs repair. The push-back against death through medicine, improvement of living conditions, and discovery of what resources creation yields to make life more dignified are linked to this biblical view, as is the need to receive an education and to establish the rule of law over human traditions, civil governments, and other forms of exploitive human power.

According to this view one looks at human existence not from the perspective of inevitable death, but from an affirmation of and struggle for life. The dust of death must be blown away by the wind of life. People stand up and get to work, hands are raised, and eyes set on a wider horizon. Minds are fed, trained, and sharpened. Laws restrain evil, while love

---

9. 1 Kgs 18 (Elijah confronts King Ahab); Acts 22:24ff (Paul rebukes the Roman centurion); Luke 13:32 (Jesus denounces Herod, that "fox").

10. The whole third chapter of Genesis is a record of God's interference with what disobedience had produced, including a new mandate for Man to put the hand to the plough in order to make life possible against an encroaching natural world.

11. John 11:33ff.

builds bridges, goes the extra mile, and dares to stand up to kings, rulers, and death itself.

The early chapters of the Bible tell us that God warned Adam and Eve against independence from him. Should they become indifferent to loving and enjoying God, and forge a new sovereign way, there would be no other world to live in. If they sought to be like God, they would lose what they had as human beings. They would die, because with such a choice they would step outside the only reality: God's already existing world. They would kill their closeness to God and become divided as people.

As the Bible tells it, God created a world in wholeness that was good, beautiful, and right. There were no conflicts then. That is obviously no longer our situation. A terrible thing happened which explains why there is a profound discontinuity between what God willed, made, and delighted in, and what exists now. By choice Adam and Eve believed a lie, something that looked attractive and desirable but could not possibly be true. They knew better, but chose to abandon what they had. They had been warned, and acted freely, not from necessity, compulsion, or example. Their world was perfect and they lacked nothing yet they were drawn to an idea (or ideal) and overlooked the real. They chose on the basis of a sensual response to something beautiful even when the temptation made no sense.[12] Their error was, above all, intellectual: they thought wrongly and carried it out with dramatic, terrible, deadly results.

They could never have been "like God," since they had been created by God. They fell for the seeming beauty of the fruit and desired equality with God, to know or "experience" both good and evil; that was their downfall. They effectively destroyed their relation with God, with each other, and with the world around them.

From then on God's creation was no longer whole. Adam and Eve created a new, painful, evil, and destructive situation when they chose a fantasy instead of believing the reality. Like the dog that opened his mouth to grab a piece of meat he saw reflected in the water and thus lost the actual meat already in his mouth, they followed an image and lost what they had. They found a wrong idea more attractive than the good reality they already enjoyed.

We all have inherited that abnormal world. Everything in our life and in nature surrounding us is marked by death, tragedy, a curse, and judgment. In this situation the Bible reaches us like letters from a distant

12. Eph 4:17ff makes the same point to each believer: sense (discernment), not sensuality (appetite), must assist moral decisions.

land. We read them to know more than what our senses tell us. Thoughtful minds outweigh sensual emotions in proper analysis. As I suggested above about Abraham,[13] the Bible speaks to our understanding, gives information, and invites us to think, reflect, weigh, and then act.

An Accumulation of Problems

What happened was not so much an angry God punishing Adam's pursuit of a wrong idea. Our first parents simply stepped off the edge of the existing world and fell. They would therefore die, body and soul. The consequence was a loss of everything they had[14] The dust of death now covers all that was meant to have the pulse of life. Relationships become difficult struggles for power.[15] Nature also becomes a burden.[16] Life now requires greater effort by the sweat of the brow or death will come even more swiftly; death will rule unless we learn and teach others the skills to resist it.

Without measurements, bridges collapse; without education, work opportunities are vastly diminished; without hygiene, sickness and death spread; without irrigation, drought and floods result; without fertilizer the harvests gradually fail; without tools, no repairs can be made; without discipline no trust or reliability can be established; without laws the powerful will exploit; without courts injustice will reign; without review rulers enforce their will with impunity, etc.

Adam and Eve's choice shattered the harmonious creation where every part was joined together perfectly. Things fall *a-part* between God and human beings, between man and woman, between mind, soul, and body, and between personal human beings and the impersonal material world. Tension, suffering, rivalry, and death, the very things God warned against, become common.

The first couple's choice to follow a false promise, an unrealizable dream, created a new reality. They went after what they thought would be perfection, and as always in life, ended up with much less than what they had before. They were deceived, lured into an unreachable ideal to

---

13. See page 33.
14. Gen 2:17 and 3:3.
15. Gen 3:12 and 16b.
16. Gen 3:17–18.

"be like God,"[17] and so became less than what Man and Woman were created to be.

The damage was both immediate and cumulative through time. It reached into every area of human life. The sin or rebellion had at least two components. The moral, legal result was that Adam and Eve became guilty and could no longer remain companions to a holy God.[18] In addition there was a material consequence with increasing severity, ending in their eventual death and affecting their children and the entire human race. Their choice so corrupted God's creation that all their descendents inherited bodies that die and hearts easily distracted by false beliefs, lies, and selfish intentions. It was all so contrary to what God made when he gave us life to be lived without interruption and forever![19]

The Bible gives us an intelligent critical perspective from outside and above the natural world. Like corrective glasses it helps us see that the real world is now problematic, containing harm and tensions, and only supporting life with much human effort and "sweat of the brow." That includes our physical body, the land we live on, the water we drink, the sicknesses our surroundings inflict, the weather patterns over us, and hidden or absent natural resources. Nature is no longer a comfortable, safe, and nourishing environment. Instead of confirming what we can know from the Bible, it reveals fractures, models no compassion, and presents a fundamental challenge to life. It adds confusing details to our search for clarity concerning knowledge of God.

Resistance to Decline, Building Walls

With this in mind we can accept God's instruction to practice dominion over nature in multiple ways. This becomes a matter of urgency. We find Cain building cities,[20] his descendents practicing animal husbandry,[21] others making music, and again others forging iron tools.[22] Nature is a creation, not a divinity. It is damaged and needs human intervention and correction to make it serviceable. We must overcome our fear of

---

17. Gen 3:4.
18. Gen 3:8, 11, 13.
19. Rom 5:12.
20. Gen 4:17.
21. Gen 4:20.
22. Gen 4:21ff

nature's dominion over us. We are not victims, contrary to what most religions reflect, but told by God to use our minds to discover ways to harness nature's resources. Abraham dug a well for irrigation, which his son continued to use to increase his harvest.[23] Nehemiah built walls for protection[24] against Israel's enemies. Roads and bridges needed maintenance for fast transport and security. Courts in each city and judges at the city gates assured faithful execution of contracts and obligations. Prophets rebuked the governments and an often false religious hierarchy. Hospitality to neighbors and the extension of legal protection over aliens were necessary to offer shelter, peace, and a shared life as people of God.

Such actions, work opportunities, and efforts encourage us all. God intends us to reduce whatever pain and threats to life we experience. We live in a dangerous world compounded by people who are not necessarily reliable or trustworthy. From panic, selfishness, or greed people willingly squeeze their fellow human beings. Through deception, and exploitation, and vengeance they try to gain an advantage even when it damages the moral and social climate for all. This is competition without compassion in a world of finite resources.

The Delight of Human Agency

But this is not the full picture of what the Bible teaches about our human condition. People are both dangerous and glorious, able to do great evil and to accomplish much that is really good. We are not left only with the present incongruity of glory and cruelty. There is the promise of a future time when God will make all things whole again, including history itself. Nature and people, both body and soul, will be renewed. Until then human agency will delay or advance that promise in real history either through neglect or through wise choices.

This longer view of history should change our attitude drastically. Sickness, death, poverty, bad government, wasted lives, unused minds, and injured human relationships should not be simply observed and counted, and justified in any way. We are not cameras that takes pictures without engagement or response. Instead, every rupture deserves and requires our interference to bring substantial healing. God calls us to rise above indifference or resignation and be agents of change to oppose

23. Gen 21:30; 26:12–15.
24. Nehemiah 2:17ff.

wrong, injustice, any form of indifference, or resignation, and naked exposure to an uncaring political or natural setting.

In other words, every situation has a factual and a moral component. What is wrong is in fact wrong in reality, not only in our personal perception, and therefore not what God intended. Painful and deadly events and the people who cause them must be recognized and judged. Nature must be examined, explored, and at times redirected to serve people first. Human agency can keep animals healthy and free from extinction, protect plants from parasites, and harness the power of water or even create rainfall for a parched land. People can meet needs with creative effort, improve what is insufficient, replace things that fail, and avoid making the same mistake several times over.

We develop products, create markets, employ and train people to serve others, and learn to live in greater security with better health and intellectual stimulation.

What simply happens is never acceptable as just a normal part of life without critical, creative analysis, and possible intervention. For none of the problems we encounter express God's will for us. It is encouraging to see that immediately after Adam and Eve hid from God in their shame, God ran after them and sought them out to give hope in a future restoration.[25] They believed God and understood the promise of the Messiah, who would be born from a future woman to remove the deep stain of death and guilt from everything. They understood their mandate to conceive children soon because they knew then that they would eventually die.[26] They worked for life against death by having children against their own demise. We are not to sink into the bosom of nature, but to follow God's ideas about nature, life, and responsibility and creatively resist all decline.

From outside of nature and history that show neither passion nor compassion, only the God of the Bible can teach a moral framework that actually facilitates life. He does not give blank orders or simply a list of commands. God's laws engage the mind and stimulate discoveries of meaning. They are not statements of power but sources of information and direction to make us think. This is in deliberate contrast to the blind obedience most religious leaders and all totalitarian governments demand. Replacing wisdom and understanding with the insistence on

---

25. Gen 3:15.

26. Gen 3:27. Notice how the emphasis is on life, not death: Eve would be "the mother of the living," without whom there would be no future woman giving birth to the Savior from guilt and death!

obedience, they turn people into mindless machines unprepared to think through variables or similar situations, who simply conform rather than being stimulated toward innovation by curiosity and free deliberation.

In daily life this impoverishes the market and impedes competition from alternative ideas, inventions, and creative enterprises. When the mind is idle, insulted, or impoverished, people rarely stand up to see what else they could do to improve their lives and that of their community.

Such responsible deliberation is also required in relation to women, whose minds and spirits are impoverished when they are seen and treated as inferior servants of men. Only Jewish and Christian ideas have seen human beings differently. In the past, Greek and Roman civilization and Chinese and Indian religions all violated the human dignity of girls and women and religious teachers and community traditions continue to do so today. They demean women by not acknowledging their real equality, where women and men are members of one single human race, of one unique "kind," because in reality "every man is born from a woman."[27] According to the Bible, man and woman are not parallel creations, but made of the same flesh, as Eve was made from Adam.

Reflection Promotes Inquiry

When more than half of all human beings, girls and women, are excluded from intelligent pursuits we all suffer from the lack of contribution, competition, critique, and challenges from people who are different yet very much like men. God does not command that exclusion. Where religious authorities insist on it, they contradict the facts on the ground. The Bible warns that "men will rule over women" as a result of sin.[28] Adam starts out immediately after the fall with such antagonism when he blames Eve for having given him the fruit to eat.[29]

Then God questions Adam and Eve instead of giving orders, to help both of them think through their situation. Questions force open a locked mind, allowing it to retrieve both hidden and forgotten knowledge. They challenge the power of imagination. "What do I do next?" stimulates each of us to imagine what might work. We then own the answer to it and arrive at an option perhaps never before considered.

27. 1 Cor 11:12.
28. Gen 3:16.
29. Gen 3:12.

God's way to change people's thoughts and values illustrates how we should interact with children, students, and employees. We use questions to look for answers instead of just quoting someone else or appealing to past practices.

Changing living situations, especially in a fallen world of hardship, depends on educated, inquisitive, courageous, and enterprising people in pursuit of what they understand to be important and true. Neither fate nor nature, neither history nor other people, can occupy the place from which you and I need to proceed diligently, in a thoughtful and circumspect manner, in order to write a new page, invent a new procedure, or start a new life.

We all need to train our minds to awaken to real challenges and help us reflect on our continuing purpose and vocation.[30] Remember that God even questions Cain to make him reconsider, to start over, and lay out in his mind what he is about to do.[31]

Our responsibility to exercise dominion is not diminished after irresponsible behavior. Our mandate to develop the land, our understanding, and our moral and intellectual life continues.[32] Life, once started, always has continuity. There is no way to step out of it and choose to live in some other world. An error does not destroy one's humanity nor diminish one's calling to have dominion now over a less than perfect situation. Failure is pardonable, yet has consequences; a sin or foolish error will result in the loss of innocence. It blunts one's arrogance, but does not destroy one's calling. We can be forgiven and start over in a different direction, though not as a different person; we always carry with us the one person we are.

We can learn additional things from God's dealing with human failure. His immediate response comes from his knowledge of the feeling of human weakness or infirmity.[33] He also knows the toughness of life and is full of compassion. Adam and Eve produced tension between themselves from shame over what they had done. Yet God does not make their marriage more difficult; instead, he instructs them to love, serve, and support each other as a couple and a team.[34]

---

30. Gen 3:9, 11, 13.
31. Gen 4:10.
32. Gen 3:16, 20.
33. Heb 4:15.
34. Gen 3:20; 4:1, 6.

God and Man at Work

God's relationship to Cain is illustrative of his fundamental refusal to abandon his investment in people or to change their calling. God does not only love good people; he shows great compassion, concern, and protective interest to all.[35] Rejecting Cain's offering because of his unbelief does not imply a rejection of him as a valuable, significant person. Even after Cain murdered his brother Abel God does not put him to death as punishment. Quite the contrary, God protects the murderer against the revenge of others.[36] God punishes the crime but does not destroy the criminal.

That does not abolish or wipe away the real consequences of his choice: he suffers exile, and has to leave his familiar piece of land, his home.[37] However, he never loses his calling, which he must now exercise elsewhere. As we saw earlier,[38] Cain starts what eventually becomes a large family, lays the foundation for a city,[39] and his children create the first musical instruments, iron tools, and animal husbandry.[40]

Later on, after the great flood, God promises not to abandon people or destroy the world. Instead he pledges to work with all humanity, using them as agents to accomplish many good things. He even uses those who are unfaithful or not part of the believing community whom he nurtures, admonishes, disciplines, and maintains as his special people.

That should lift our spirits and energize our determination. We have received much as human beings with minds and hands. With such a high calling, we must put our abilities to work to reduce the failings and the unhappy and often unfair experiences of others in a fallen, damaged world. We must now see how that can be achieved.

---

35. Gen 4:6–7.
36. Gen 4:15–16.
37. Gen 4:14, 16.
38. See page 61.
39. Gen 4:17.
40. Gen 4:20–22.

Chapter 8

Everyone a Craftsman

FIRST, WHAT A RELIEF that we do not have to pretend that life is in any way easy or normal, or that this is the best of all possible worlds! It is full of challenges that require hard physical and mental work. Dangers lurk on every side. There is much to teach each new generation and much for them to learn.

Second, *what a relief* that our situation is not always deserved due to personal fault and guilt, nor is it terminally hopeless as a result of prior personal wrong. Neither is it part of the design of an impersonal destiny, fate, or unknown evil forces.

Third, *what a relief* that we are honored as persons, given work to do and dominion to exercise as God's stewards in his good creation. It is an active, enterprising assignment. As God provides defined forms for each part of his creation,[1] we fulfill our calling as human agents for life through purposeful work and loving attention to God, to other people, and to the natural world. That is what God envisaged, though the execution has become much more difficult.

So we must set out to be fully human to ourselves and the world around us. We should honor every person as our neighbor[2] and make an effort to relieve his hardships. In the Jewish and Christian understanding, each person is uniquely made in the image of God and loved by him. As people who think, act, and feel we are more like God than anything else in our world.

When God became a human being and received a human body from a woman, Mary, and entered our time and space in real history, he

---

1. Job 38:39–41, Ps 104.
2. Luke 10:25ff.

took on the form, appearance, and characteristics familiar to us. He is not an elephant, a holy cow, a mighty tiger, the malaria-carrying tsetse fly, or any king of the jungle. He is not a shaman or the night wind, the flood water, sun, or moon. He is a person, and to show that God really exists and loves he took on a human form that was already in his own divine image from the beginning, and became man.

That is wonderful but not altogether surprising. Human persons were made in the image of the eternal person God to begin with. When God came to earth as Jesus of Nazareth he did not become something essentially different from us, for we too are persons, unlike the natural things around us. We think, feel, and act, because we have received these characteristics or attributes from the person "God" of the Bible. Nature functions and produces, but people live.

From God to People on Earth

God is not an idea that humans have projected from wishful thinking or psychological need. That has sometimes been suggested,[3] but it leaves the crucial question unanswered: how did human beings with a need to invent a god, as is often suggested, come about in the first place? No, the sequence of cause and effect moves the other way: God precedes all else, he is "the first cause." God had the idea to add people into a world of real things like water, stones, shrubs, and animals—so here we are, not only things, but people surrounded by things!

This voids the unanswered question why people developed a need to invent a god. The Bible tells us that God invented people and that is why we are god-like[4] in our ability to think, to understand, and to choose rightly or wrongly. That is also why life for Adam without Eve, and for contemporary Man existence without God, is so lonely, unfulfilling, and cruel.

I said above that it is a great relief to affirm and embrace our essential calling to be nothing more and nothing less than human beings. That is also exactly what we are according to our personal experience, neither beast nor angel. We must reject religious views that take away our humanity and tell people to lie low, think less, and learn to follow the crowd and

---

3. By modern materialists like Feuerbach and Marx, or psycho-analysts like Freud.

4. Psalms and Jesus (John 10:31) call people "gods" because we are able to understand and apply God's words to life. Anthropomorphic terms can apply to God, because God has made the anthropos in his image.

the flow of events. We must also reject reductionist views in the natural sciences about an emerging world that tell us we are merely the sum total of prior material and complex genetic information, with the daily addition of the food we digest. As it is, we are neither body-less spirits nor spirit-less bodies. Neither is a sufficient explanation of what it means to be a person. We all have an outer body and an inner life of the mind.

Historically, the Bible's proposition that men and women are in the image of God freed people from the prison of their cultural and religious views. They could embrace a more energizing view of significant and responsible human life. Without the Bible, the firmament above or the smallest particle within constitutes the limit of what can be known and what defines us. With the Bible we are introduced to a God whose nature and personality alone explain the existence of the universe in its orderly form as well as what makes human beings so different. The stars with their steady movement in heaven are clearly a part of creation and not the creator; to the matter he had already created God added a "breath of life" to make us people, who are much different, "living souls."

An Increasingly Complex Reality

The human significance of each individual is thus established and real history becomes possible. Each of us matters significantly. Unlike a stone thrown into water we cause ripples that never stop. The Bible's proposition that God took time to create the start of an increasingly complex reality demonstrates the value of effort and skill. So too we can elaborate what needs doing, make plans, and work to execute them. We can train patiently to become more skillful and admire those who are further ahead with their achievements. We can learn from them to overcome our own weaknesses and build on the improved knowledge of others who precede us.

This suggests that real value is not only in the finished product or at the conclusion of a process, but in the application of effort at every step along the way. God loves and favors us from the beginning; we do not receive his approbation or attention only at the end of life for the things that were accomplished, as others might give a reward for years of service. The means matter to God and are valued from the start because they already serve the desired end of people being at work all along. In the same way we do not become people only when we become important or recognized; we are people from conception forward and we cannot become anything else!

The rightfulness of working is the foundation for our whole outlook on the value of invention, discovery, schooling, design studies, and even polls to discover people's needs and desires. The idea of entrepreneurship comes from the French, "to step in, to take, to interfere, accomplish"; the English term is "to undertake"— to take up something and do it. We have a goal in mind and we take time to reach it, however long the task requires. The relation, and at times tension, between what exists in our hands and what we imagine between our ears frees creative energy. It drives us to achieve what began as an image, a wish, a desire in our mind, an urgency to meet a need. Skillful hands then shape that image into an external, material form.

Just as God did not create in one single act all at once, with one powerful word, so also do we go through steps of accomplishment and continuous refinement. We need neither stop with the first attempt nor be dissatisfied with it. The first of many failures may be the best we can do at that time but it sets us on the path to seek improvements. Frustration frames a continuous challenge. It is not a punishment, just like an evaluation in school indicates our present level of skills and does not define our personality or full potential. When life and abilities expand along a continuous line, every step along the way contributes to greater achievement even without always reaching the imagined end.

Such continuous existence and effort describes life now and also when God will make all things whole again. The heavenly city Jerusalem will be a place of continuous activity and forever unfinished, vibrant and not static. The Bible portrays it as dynamic, with human existence restored and every now so familiar error removed.

Contrary to Plato's ideal forms of eternal perfection, the Bible speaks of a continuum of accomplishment in space and time. Instead of Plato's changeless world of justice and beauty, the Bible speaks of just acts and beautiful lives, of making things right again at every step. The life of the Son of God, Jesus, was active, engaged, creative, with the pleasures of a wedding feast, teaching, and healing. This is the opposite of Buddha's state of happiness expressed in permanently grinning statues. A static or perfected existence would make creative life, and thereby personality, come to an end.

The Forever Unfinished Business

Throughout life now and later our skills gradually improve, and every stage has its own degree of perfection, justification, praise, and satisfaction.

The business of life is eternally unfinished. Tomorrow comes, in part, as the result of today's choices. There is openness in our freedom of initiative, invention, and action. We have the sovereignty derived from God to give shape and direction to history. This view is distinct from the common belief in many cultures that whatever is already there is all that was meant to be, either by divine design or spiritual power. This view common to most religions, including secular materialism, leads eventually to passivity. Each circumstance is the inevitable consequence of prior conditioning by gods, the stars in heaven, or one's genetic inheritance. "This moment was meant to be, it could not have been otherwise," they might say. The future is already designed and will inevitably happen.

No Place for Simple Repetition

Only the Bible envisions reality characterized by continual dynamic change without conflict. This is completely unlike the Greek universe of finished perfection or static sameness. The Bible has no ideal of justice, beauty, or goodness once and for all, as Plato and other Greek thinkers proposed. Instead, all of history, including what takes place in the presence of God in heaven, results from genuine choice: first by God, then men and women made in his image, as well as whoever else has a mind and acts accordingly, such as angels (there is also Satan, whose intention is evil).

Change is written into the short overview of the original creation in Genesis.[5] It is intended when we are urged to have dominion and rule, to till the garden and name the animals, to become couples and bear children. All these activities leave marks and alter the present into something new as they change in real time what was there before. Change is the result of activity, of thought and implementation, the consequence of what we undertake. There can be neither personality nor life without change in history.

The contrary emphasis on repetition and conformity comes from belief in repeated cycles. In this view history is like a womb without anything ever being born. It is like the earth revolving under the fixed

---

5. Gen 1.

firmament of stars. All is mathematics with no art when people accept whatever is with resignation: things are and remain what they have always been. In this form of traditionalism, patterns in nature or in the human past are assumed to be the best of all things, the only way. They must be repeated in each generation. Justice, goodness, and beauty are fixed ideals rather than qualities of personal choices and creative acts.

However, the Bible tells us that history is a record of what happened, including what happened unnecessarily.[6] We all inherit it, in the sense that we cannot affect the past and must live in its consequences. But each of us can start now to alter it and contribute something else from today forward. History is an ongoing record of events that did not need to happen but were chosen at some point, wisely or foolishly, by choice makers like us. Now it is our turn. Perfection is not achieved when everything stands still, once and for all, but rather it is manifest at each stage when something good, just, and beautiful is accomplished.

Since the reality of change is found in Biblical teaching we should not be surprised that it is confirmed in every aspect of reality. It is in the chemical processes of plants extracting nutrients from soil or fish taking oxygen out of the water in which they swim! A changeless world exists only in some people's belief, but belief by itself does not indicate truth. Anything is believable to the person who does not require evidence or verification and who doesn't practice critical thinking and review. Perhaps the first case of blind belief was Adam and Eve, who believed they could "be like God," driven by desire rather than reflection. It was an idea impossible in reality. Likewise, many believed for a long time that white people were a superior race when in fact there is only one human race. Some believe in a god who remains unmoved and unbound by his own moral character, who can act at will and control all things regardless of contradictions. Each case is an illustration of a belief without evidence in either reality or Scripture.

Change through effort, will, and courageous determination is essential to the biblical perspective. It forms the intellectual base of such realities as free markets, government with the consent of the governed, the rule of law, polyphonic symphonies, and educated citizens with tools to resist and correct this indifferent and often hostile world. Biblical teaching bears fruit wherever it is applied, with much practical benefit to daily life.

---

6. See *Neither Necessary nor Inevitable: History Needn't Have Been Like That,* by Udo Middelmann (Wipf and Stock, 2011).

Many authorities in all walks of life fear the affirmation of individual choice in the Bible. They prefer that people accept their leadership blindly, without questioning the intellectual or moral grounds for their claims of unalterable authority. They require everyone to accept and obey their policies, constantly repeating ideological slogans, religious incantations, and spiritual mantras tied to their office.

The God of the Bible, the author of his creation, speaks from knowledge and with passion, but never with such authoritarian intent.[7] He desires that humans act, create, and invent. He told Adam and Eve to be fruitful and multiply.[8] What more dramatic way to change the face of the earth and the flow of history than to give birth to another human being! Each of us has a unique name identity and is forever valued as a distinct human being, even when we later disappoint because of what we do with inherited or created opportunities in our lives.[9]

The God introduced in the Bible nurtures this open attitude to life by encouraging inquiry, invention, and a lively effort of the mind to consider alternatives. The only limits are the form and function of the real world and the consequences of people's past choices. One of *my* limits is that I cannot sing in the opera with my untrained vocal cords; no one can drive safely when drunk; you cannot have your cake and eat it too; events during the tenth century cannot be undone by later generations.

That is why, according to the Bible, we should see all of life as unfinished business. Past choices set boundaries but today and tomorrow are created by what you and I accomplish within those boundaries and thereby broaden them. We can step out of the prison of repetition or the security of others' approval to become real people, learning skills and exercising dominion as image bearers of God. We are free to create history, new products and markets, solutions for people's lives, and order through laws that define and limit the wrongful use of human imagination.

This factual world of definitions, reliable information, and stable forms is open to our exploration. Careful observation tells us ever more about how reality is constructed and what various things can be used for and how they interact. Nature and history are filled with resources to be applied and rightly exploited in pursuit of a purposeful dominion. We

---

7. Jesus says that when people do not heed his words, the very stones will speak.
8. Gen 1:28.
9. Notice how 1 Chron starts with eight chapters of names, woven around and attached to a genealogy of the promised Christ. All are related, very distant cousins, and none is forgotten or overlooked by God as unimportant in some corner of the world.

can thoroughly study this world and how it works. We should stop being victims and become craftsmen, masters, knowledgeable people accountable to God and others.

Confidence in a Reasonable World

The Bible gives us assurance that behind the unknown is the not-yet-known of a defined reality, where everything is "according to its kind." It affirms a steady definition to things, an internal rationality and logic, which we can confirm through careful discovery. God does not play dice with the universe.[10] This proposition requires our intelligent study of creation if we are to gain mastery over everything in it. Through thoughtful inquiry we can research the hidden workings of the world and replace former secrets with verifiable knowledge about its substance and behavior. Reliable information about the regular functions of the material world will become more precise and detailed, remaining true over time and not changing on someone's whim or faith. Gathered from many sources at different times, these details build a grid of mutually supporting evidence and increasing insight into a trustworthy material world.

There are reasons for all things. Chemical and physical properties determine the material content, the internal strength, and the predictable function of everything. Each metal melts at a specific level of heat, stones have a measurable static strength, and plastics are waterproof. Concrete will hold up for years when the right mixture of cement, sand, and stone produces the necessary chemical bond. Certain soils will nourish diverse plants. There is a cause and effect reality to God's creation, so that nothing is the result of occult personalities, spiritual forces, or random events in or behind nature.

We are creative and productive human beings made in the image of God, who live in a material, impersonal world full of things we should use wisely. Intelligence, careful observation, logical calculation, and a love for details are required and encouraged to figure out how and why things like wood and metal, water and soil, molecules and bacteria, fertilizer and air always function the way they do.

By definition, a craftsman is a person who has the ability and power (*craft* comes from the Germanic word *Kraft*, meaning *power*) to exert dominion with knowledge in his thoughts and skill in his hands. The

---

10. The phrasing of this idea is attributed to Albert Einstein.

craftsman's calling is to observe, study, and then apply detailed knowledge in response to life's challenges. He is enjoined to improve his skills, practice proper techniques, make factual observations, and share explanations with everyone. Work may be slow; it may well take years and, indeed, should never end. It grows and gives much satisfaction through frequent practice. It requires an observing eye, critical discernment, a careful and detailed memory, and a mind that sees possible connections before they exist in the external world. Every craftsman is first an intellectual who has thought about efficient ways to use objects and materials, even though he is working mostly with his hands rather than his pen or mouth.

A good and careful craftsman acquires tacit knowledge, a self-conscious awareness of possibilities, a repertoire of procedures that have become second nature to him or her. Routines are refined through rational and relational thinking about the practical use of materials. No longer satisfied with "good enough," the craftsman stops "muddling through" and applies skills developed through face-to-face encounters with people, materials, and problems to find solutions from his or her knowledge capital.

It can be argued that the craftsman uses his mind far more than many office workers and those who work with computer data in government employment.[11] A craftsman has to make intelligent, costly decisions rather than follow blindly the dictates of a program or the orders of a distant boss. Manual competence is derived and refined from an intellectual competence about the material world from based on systematic encounters with the ways of nature and the material world. With his secure grasp, the craftsman is actually transforming the world through work and thereby extricates himself from dependence on obscure forces, superstitious notions, or random moments of success.

An Ennobling Culture

Wherever the Bible is taught and considered it lays the foundation for certainties we can test and use to improve our life. It presents to our mind's eye larger possibilities than we face immediately on any day so that our

---

11. This is the proposition of Matthew B. Crawford in his book *Shop Class as Soulcraft: An inquiry into the Value of Work* (Penguin, 2010). It contains also a fascinating description of the intellectual work of craftsmen.

understanding about creation can grow. It stretches the horizon of our mental world, nurtures imagination, and invites exploration of alternatives.

In this way the Bible creates a culture that respects the nobility of the human being. It encourages a curious, compassionate, conscientious outlook, not a hands-off mentality of responding to a mysterious world with hesitation and fear, with limits to what can be repaired in our painful human existence.

Individuals and cultures without such a proposition of things working "according to their kind" do not have the same confidence of gaining and exercising dominion. As long as all sorts of contrary events are assumed to be inevitable, unpredictable, and outside of an overarching framework, there is no certainty of a steady world with defined characteristics. Where the Bible has been taught and people have begun to understand its truth about all the areas of life it touches on, people manage life better than they do without it.

Neglected Minds Impoverish Lives

Individuals and societies without the Bible as an intelligible text have difficulty in thinking abstractly and making judgments about what happens in the world. Both abilities are needed to bridge the distance between what is and what could or ought to be. This is true not only on the level of missing content or explanations, which the Bible provides; in addition, recent research into the way the human brain works indicates that exposure to a text requiring understanding, not just hearing, helps the brain think abstractly and logically and raise questions.

When there is no text or little face-to-face conversation to engage the mind, the development of the physical brain is dramatically slowed and even stifled, making it difficult to function logically and to reason things through.[12]

Events just happen as immediate impressions without explanation or context. An impression by itself, whether it comes from the immediate situation of life or some powerful elders, spirits or gods and without the critical rational tools necessary to understand its value in context, creates a powerful and unquestioned authority which may or may not be true.

---

12. For research into the brain development of young children see Jane Healey's *Endangered Minds: Why Children Don't Think and What We Can Do About It* (Simon and Schuster, 1999).

Everyone a Craftsman

When young children learn through answers and statements recited in unison from memory, in a group as a collective performance, rational discernment suffers. Where no explanation is given, no error considered and discussed, and no alternative imagined, the child's mind is handicapped by the limits of a poorly developed brain. Rote learning gives the impression of knowledge but provides no understanding of how it was arrived at or why it is true.

I have found that this rote method of teaching is widespread in schools in cultural settings where the Bible's propositions are unknown or openly rejected. Many Bengali and formerly Soviet Russian schools favor the mindless repetition of answers expressed in the collective of many children speaking in unison. Both Islamic religious obedience and materialist authoritarian ideology demand conformity rather than encouraging curiosity. But the individual child deserves to be given tools to learn the reason behind the answers. Recitation from memory is not an indication of something having been discovered, discerned, and understood. It only expresses obedience, not comprehension. It produces the pleasure of belonging but hinders the development of an individual's humanity.

By contrast, a mind trained to understand a text, a sentence, or a paragraph will delay reaching a conclusion until the various parts—subject, verb, object, dependent clauses and pronouns—are put together to form an understandable and comprehensible (from Latin: *com* and *prehendere*: to hold together, to seize, to take) whole that is part of a complex reality. A mind exposed only to pictures, isolated facts, commands, or a chorus of identical answers does not respond analytically.

A picture is mostly seen. It makes an impression and needs no comprehension or understanding. It creates a visual sensation but does not awaken the mind to explore verifiable, sensible explanations. When seeing something momentarily, untrained minds do not make connections and discover causes. The interaction of cause and effect, the prior choices of people leading up to the pictured scene, the chemical reactions and physical forces of nature remain unnoticed, so that authority is never questioned.[13] People remain superstitious and interpret events

---

13. Abstract thinking, i.e. imagining a hypothetical situation, is required to understand why one needs to change the oil in a well-running motor before the engine freezes up and then breaks. Afterwards it is too late. Seeing the need for an oil change is part of a longer process that includes facts and reflections, the present and the future, plus skill and responsibility to prevent a potentiality from ever becoming an actuality. Once the motor dries up, everything is too late.

without insight, settling for any random claims of authority. The benefit of critical evaluation as an intellectual consequence to the proposition that God created an orderly world remains distant. Drawn to sensations but untrained to make sense of them, they ignore the call to create a life with the obligation to act responsibly to themselves, their children, and the world in its given form.

Knowledge can and should increase, like one building block on top of another, to construct a more complete picture of how nature works, or what makes a society just, or what makes an argument cohere. There is a fundamental logic in every aspect of this cause and effect world. The only "random" events are due to unpredictable human choices. For, while everything works "according to its kind" in the natural world and always functions steadily, the human world is untidy, often crooked, and just as easily pleasing as disappointing.

A single event in isolation has always given individuals something true: whatever it was, it happened. But only the discipline to discover how single events recur and how they relate to others can provide good explanations in a wider context. As David Deutsch says, explanations are "fundamental descriptions of the world. A decent explanation has universal reach, and the quest for explanations is what makes people human. Identifying good explanations constitutes progress. And because there is no particular limit to what can be explained, explanations are infinite."[14]

End to Humiliation

The desire for knowledge is part of being human. From it grew the wider scientific culture of critical inquiry. This thirst to know is behind all explorations of the mind and across land, sea, air, and space. It is vital for finding good explanations through correcting errors and has led to astounding discoveries as people have sought to satisfy their insatiable thirst for more knowledge.

Biblical assertions constitute one such thirst-quenching explanation because they establish links and relationships to truth in central areas of human inquiry and common experience. They are not just opinion, but rather

---

14. For this and the next quotation see David Deutsch's *The Beginning of Infinity: Explanations That Transform the World* (Viking Press, 2011), and the review of it in *The Economist*, March 28, 2011.

real truth, simple and elegant, explaining related phenomena and putting each in its proper place within a larger logical and verifiable structure.

David Deutsch claims that "mankind is only just at the beginning of an almost everlasting journey of creating explanations of the world." Inquiry, of which science is one method, expresses multiple questions and must itself be questioned. According to the Bible, inquiry is part of God's mandate to work in creation, to have dominion in the form of good explanations, to inform moral and political philosophy and even aesthetics.

The Bible's influence replaces "religious belief," widespread superstition, and elaborate guessing games with verifiable, reasonable knowledge gained from logic and practical experimentation. The long-term consequence of people discovering that the Bible allows, even demands, the study of a world in which each created bit is "made according to its kind" is increased insight into all aspects of the universe. Rational procedures lead to coherent and steady explanations for what exists and how things happen. Christianity is *not* against knowledge;[15] it was only at the time of the European Enlightenment, with people turning away from God, that an opposition between belief and knowledge developed.

Again, the move from blind religious faith to knowledge does not originate from a rejection of Christianity and the embrace of a naturalist or materialist perspective. It actually arose out of Biblical truth *to* the human mind wherever it was set free from various ideologies which tried to cap it. The Bible alone furnished the intellectual encouragement to look at a larger reality, an interrelated world of things and people functioning according to their kind. The Enlightenment and the rise of natural science had anti-religious partners but were initially not anti-Christian at all. In fact, many early scientists worked toward a coherent understanding of the mind of God in setting up an accessible creation.

Like the Bible itself, the new scientific view admitted only the criteria of verifiable truth while rejecting authoritarian pronouncements, whether from religion or state. Most of the early natural scientists were, as Christian believers, freed from bondage to fear, superstition, and

---

15. Based on a deliberately twisted understanding of Gen 3:5, because "knowledge" in Jewish thought is more concerned with immediate experience than facts in the rational intellect. I suggested earlier (page 29) that Adam was forbidden to have the *experience* of evil, though he certainly had the factual knowledge of it, since God had told him that it would be death, the destruction of all he currently had: fullness of life.

unquestioned religious views imposed from distant and often muddled traditions.[16] They were scientists precisely because they were Christians.

A More Purposeful Effort

Even before the first scientific academies were founded in the sixteenth century, the teaching from the Bible encouraged earlier believers to respond to painful, cruel, often catastrophic circumstances by forming communities of intent with an outlook to take charge rather than suffer. After the sacking of Rome in the fifth century and the resultant collapse of civic order, thoughtful individuals who saw the Bible's teaching in relation to all of life worked for greater peace and security. In a time of murder, pillaging, and destruction they sought protection against marauding tribes through the security of walled cities and monastic communities. Gradually cities set up market rules and courts; from there they went out to pacify the surrounding villages and countryside.

Institutions of trained specialists encouraged education of the mind through teaching, sermons, careful observation of nature, and the copying of old texts in a safe environment. Schools and universities were founded for the study of law to bring order to conflicts, set the framework for market behavior, and govern contracts and the weight and quality of products. Hospitals brought medicine and healing to hurt bodies,[17] developing new ways to improve public health, water quality, and general hygiene in hospitals and at home.[18] Long before the invention of mechanical clocks, hours were established within each day and church bells marked the passage of time so that workers could determine when to work instead of wasting time in idle delay.

Moral instruction to the mind and the creation of markets, cities, and schools gradually transformed the way people related to one another. Frequent reminders of the biblical calling of man led to practical consequences in much of public life, including the development of crafts

---

16. Much Greek/Platonic thought muddled Christianity for more than a thousand years. Also consider scholasticism, which weakened appreciation of the real world in favor of the world beyond where the soul aims to reside.

17. The ducal hospital in Beaune, France, was constructed directly over a creek to flush away soiled bandages.

18. Brewing of beer and distillation of herbs and fruits used the medicinal effects of alcohol on bacteria. St. Paul had already told Timothy, "use a little wine for (the) stomach" (1 Tim 5:23).

among a wide circle of people. A craft is a specific skill learned over time to master an unfinished task for the enrichment of life. The abundant variety of crafts in technical fields as well as in the arts, law, medicine, and psychology, requires mental and manual skills sensitive to the order in things and the human person. By expressing refinement and efficiency in pursuit of a specific purpose or to overcome a hindrance, craftsmen improve life for everyone.

A craft does not simply occur. It is an effort to embellish life while reducing its pain and frustration through discernment and growing ability. Craftspeople deeply explore a systematic engagement with the material world to learn the characteristics and usefulness of materials. As masters of their skill they express a profound refusal to be overcome or ruled by circumstances, indifference, impersonal nature, and death. Crafts share with other life activities a deliberate effort to advance, to not stand still. In this way crafts are like love, poetry, a sculpture, or someone's clothes and the home they live in; they are like working for peace and justice in politics, the protection of people and property in business, employment opportunities, and the creation of needed objects. A work of craftsmanship leaves a statement of human uniqueness and purposeful accomplishment that lasts beyond one's own eventual death.

A craftsperson is always a unique individual who marks his space and time with his accomplishments and name. His work is a testimony to his humanity and to the transforming power of work. It is a visible display of how an originally subjective, abstract idea can take on greater permanence beyond death.

Such work gives individuals the experience of being actors, agents.[19] They are active representatives of human existence with the competence to place a lasting product, object, or social reality into a changing and forgetful world. They do something well for its own sake from a gradually increasing repertoire of procedures. Using their particular skill and expressing their unique calling, craftspeople get deeply into their work because they want to use the best materials for a particular purpose. They produce something durable that makes the world more familiar and reduces our feeling of insecurity about the basic character of reality.

Through their agency, craftspeople recognize and share their humanity with others. Their work not only teaches us about diligence, the reality of time and patience, the importance of learning from trial and

---

19. For some of these ideas I am indebted to Matthew B. Crawford, *Shop Class as Soulcraft: An Inquiry into the Value of Work* (Penguin, 2010).

error; it also leave us with things more permanent than personal moments and experiences. Normal changes in the flow of history are arrested for a while in the craft object. Like a seam that binds different cuts of cloth into a suit or dress, an object holds together a longer measure of time, from raw material to finished product, helping everyone to see the world as more reliable.

Individual craftsmanship has been the source of new machinery, patents, and whole companies like Singer sewing machines, Ford and Mercedes Benz cars, Bosch instruments, Zeiss lenses, and Ericsson telephones. They carry the name and design of individual craftspeople. Bricks for building and tiles for roofs, pottery dishes and furniture all bear the stamp of the place where they are baked or made. In the past, machines often also bore decorative additions that have no function other than to please and to embellish. These remain like the signatures of artists, signs of unashamed daring, effort, and success.

We should all be able to look at what we have done and affirm that in spite of frequent mistakes and frustrating imperfection we are satisfied with what we have created. The physical, exacting manipulation of material should reveal the aesthetic sensitivity and bear the stamp of the cognitive awareness of a particular person. Craftspeople are specialists, singled out by their drive, motivation, and particular accomplishments. From their wealth of careful practices they create the capital of specialized knowledge that can be passed on to the next generation.

Without the mentality of true craftsmanship someone may still be able to build a simple shelter against the weather or a thorny hedge against night prowlers. Neighbors can simply follow the model and construct their own, without attention or concern for increasing skill or preference. Yet when whatever is, is good enough, then no specific craft is exhibited, no specialization into other fields is explored, and there is little improvement from one generation to another. The scope of an individual's activity remains indistinguishable from that of a neighbor. The community then stands still in a changeless present. Bondage to tradition and fear of novelty reign, reflecting a mindset that sees existence as cyclical rather than progressive. It is intolerant of any difference that might produce envy, jealousy, and competition;[20] however, that same intolerance also diminishes the possibility of competence and valuable improvements.

---

20. Marxist-Leninism promised this as characteristic of a society in which private property was abolished.

When forced to follow a plan, to be wrapped into a social or religious collective without review or improvement, one is a slave to a common course within inevitable historic necessity. Many Soviet citizens lived under that dictate, as do many in tribal societies with a collective religious and social mindset. The masters, whether termites, flood and fire, or the party and its pronouncements, control all of life. If imperfection is ideologically or religiously inadmissible, the current situation is inevitably considered better than any alternative.

Every Effort Brings Benefits

Improvements come mostly by the determined efforts of individuals and inventors whose minds are open to alternatives. Their skills free the next person to find other problems to solve in an area of their specific expertise and competence. Specialization creates mutual dependence and appreciation, and sets all people free to pursue additional challenges. Otherwise, when special skills and callings are not recognized from fear that someone's unique human abilities will stand out, life and its opportunities are neglected and wasted.

Once again, the Bible's view of things "according to their kind" matches what we find in the stability of form and function, the predictability of performance, and the usefulness of even partial knowledge. Reality is discovered to be reliable, from both experience and explanation. Knowledge accumulated over many years yields rich rewards. We can add to it, correct false insights, and learn from mistakes and bad consequences. Knowledge, unless it is continuously pursued, will be lost through neglect; it must be constantly reviewed, understood, valued, and applied to see its practical benefits.

Ancient Roman technology illustrates this clearly. Cisterns were carved out in Egypt to store water for irrigation during dry periods. In northern regions of the Empire, Romans had central heating, using smoke to warm the floors and lead hot water radiators to warm the air. They knew how to build strong walls of concrete rather than mud or wood. Skills like these were lost, forgotten over generations of neglect, because people did not maintain that knowledge or gave it up in the European Middle Ages for an otherworldly spirituality that turned the focus of life from earth to heaven.

The Inca in Peru built irrigation canals to bring water from the highlands of the Andes to the coastal desert. Through neglect, foreign conquest, and fatalistic religions, all that remains are potsherds on the ground, ruins of former settlements, and traces of disintegrating canal walls. The desert has won again because subsequent generations gave up and failed to maintain a once prosperous civilization.

The wealth and high culture of the kingdom of Mali, with its elaborate irrigation systems, could not overcome the influence of fatalistic religions when natural conditions deteriorated after the thirteenth century. Timbuktu became synonymous with "the far end of the world."

Specifically People

I come back to the assertion that people are made "according to their kind," but a kind specifically different from nature. Made in the image of a loving and imaginative God, we are choice-makers, inventive, challenged and driven to create: called to be human. We can count on the stability of the natural world around us, reason with it, and take advantage of it. Fearful and fatalistic beliefs and passive responses can be successfully countered with answers from our humanity and the Bible; in both we find motivation for greater skills and purposeful lives. This outlook awakens responsible human creativity, helping to diminish the pain of life.

In the biblical view, we all have some choice in crafting our own lives. We can either lie low, flat on the ground, or raise our eyes to see further ahead. Even when standing upright on solid ground we remain immobile until we lift one foot and set it in front of the other. Only then can we move ahead!

We all start from a certain place on earth and we are all linked to our own time. But we are free to develop alternative thoughts; we transcend the limits of the real with our minds. We can take wing like an eagle, benefiting from enriched ideas and receiving satisfaction from being *unlike* silent nature. Remaining "flat on the ground" intertwines us with the push and shove of natural settings, group thinking, and the whims of others. Rising above that in our minds, we take our first steps by questioning the reality of what is in the light of what we wish it were, or what it ought to be. Only then are we able to freely admit a problem, state our dissatisfaction, complain about our previous failure, and start to look for and implement solutions.

You will recall the old Jewish saying I referred to earlier. It raises these questions: If you are not going to act, then what? If not now, when? If not you, who? These questions assume that life is never accomplished and problems remain unsolved. Humans are not tied down but stand at the beginning of a road, free to walk on to get somewhere. In walking on that road we should be morally sensitive and psychologically independent. We should be accusers of what is wrong, resist the status quo, and always ask: What else can be done? What other needs should be addressed? What are the central problems that prevent our advance, threaten our safety, destroy our food, or create tension among people? What skills should I learn, and what task is better done by someone else? How can the work best be divided among a company of skillful workers?

A Dramatic Contrast

A stark and powerful contrast exists between most religions and ideologies on one hand and biblical propositions on the other. The former may contain beautiful images of harmony and promises of future progress, of an ideal world of permanent satisfaction, but they are only inventions of the mind, make-believe dreams, which demand adherents hold to something that exists only in their belief, regardless of how reality functions.

Such a belief has power over people's lives by creating a community of obedient followers who hope expectantly in a future paradise in heaven or on earth without considering whether their faith is accurate, verifiable, and sensibly coherent in the present. Religion and ideology exert a powerful pull over people by means of symbols, practices, and common visions in order to create a community free from present doubt and open conflict. Priests and rulers use formal celebrations, lofty words, and pious attitudes to unite a people. The effect calms like an opiate. Karl Marx saw such a drug in all religions but did not admit that his own belief in the progress of an impersonal history was just as much a religion. Its purpose was to restrain people and normalize their current condition, to prevent them from raising questions in hope of finding real answers to genuine problems.

Religion lulls the intelligence and masks genuine pain with the comfort of conformity and an escape into resignation. Religion both agitates and dominates a community; it does not necessarily answer questions about life's purpose, meaning, or morals.

The contrast to religions is found where God's Scriptures give accurate understanding and explanations of the real world. Faith does not create it so. Christian faith is belief based on good and sufficient evidence that God exists as a personality, is truthful, and generous. God's instructions through the prophets and apostles contain insights and explanations, not hidden fantasies or insults to the human mind, heart, and body.[21] The Bible is a book of information, not of repudiation.

Ethics and Morality That Make Sense

Biblical ethics and morality are also related to the shape of creation. Its moral laws do not indicate authoritarian control. They are stated and defined on the basis of the natural, logical, life or death consequences of choices. They do not represent a despot's desire that his people conform and obey. Rather, moral directives in the Bible establish a practical reference to how creation functions. God's laws are the outline of what is right and true, and therefore have beneficial consequences. They reveal what is true in the sense that one can speak of a well-built wall being true to the structural requirements of its purpose, and true to earth's pull of gravity. When the laws of physics are broken the wall falls down.

God's laws describe a world with lasting, trustworthy definitions. Water will always run downhill; it follows a natural law. People by their nature will always invent and remain puzzling. Their next decision originates at any moment and is unknown to anyone until then. It is not the natural result of prior influences. Since the law governing their nature, their "natural law", is to be free to make choices, people need a moral orientation from external sources. Laws in the Bible are given to remind us that there are limits to faulty imagination in the real world. They draw the line between what is merely thought and what is already fixed so that no thought can alter it.

The primary example of such a law reestablishing an already existing reality against the vanity of inventions is the so-called Great Command, which sums up all the Law and the Prophets:[22] To love God with heart, mind, soul, and strength,[23] and your neighbor as yourself.[24] The

---

21. Heb 11:1,7.
22. Matt 22:40.
23. Deut 6:5.
24. Lev 19:18.

reality re-awakened by the command is human life in a personal universe where God is Creator, people are my neighbors, and love should characterize all relationships.

That Great Command is then elaborated in greater detail to prevent any vague sentimentality about love. Love is a series of specific choices enumerated in the Ten Commandments.[25] The command to have no God but the one who brought Israel out of Egypt is linked to the proposition that there is no other God whose existence and character explain the form of the real world and the mannishness of Man. Every other god is an invention, either the human projection of a wishful idea or a dreaded, fearful image quite unrelated to the facts of reality.

In the same way, we are told to honor father and mother because without them we ourselves would not even exist. We should not steal because things belong to someone through their effort. Stealing property, time, or trust is a form of pretending: I pretend that I made, own, or inherited what I hold. The Sabbath is a day of rest because it reminds us that we are made in the image of God and should not live like everything else does in and by its nature, as though every day were the same. Giving false witness assumes that reality is not defined, but created by our words, witness, and wily behavior.

The awareness of original, lasting, and reasonable definitions in the created world enables us to speak of fair judgments, right behavior, and true weights and measures. Facts are fixed, not socially variable and tentatively accepted. A pound by definition has a certain weight and a quart a certain volume. What is born of a human parent is always a human being. When Jesus says that our "yes" should mean "yes" and our "no" be a "no," he demands that a word be descriptive of a fact. Swearing by God's name is of no value unless the factual truth is told, and then swearing is unnecessary. No oath should be needed to give weight to a truth claim;[26] and no oath makes a falsehood right! Jesus demands that we tell the truth at all times. No religious dressing up makes something more true or reliable.

This is what Jesus means when he says that our righteousness should exceed that of the Pharisees, the religious teachers of his time.[27] The Septuagint of the Old Testament uses the same word for righteous-

---

25. Exod 20:2–17 and Deut 5:6–21.
26. Matt 5:34.
27. Matt 5:20.

ness when it describes the requirement for honest or righteous standards, scales, and measures.[28]

Where the Bible is used to instruct people about the nature of the universe it gives personal and intellectual confidence that life has a purpose: we are loved and wanted by the creator; he has a moral character and is therefore reliable; he created this world with a specific form so that we can gather information and make good choices based on knowledge. God also tells us in the Bible that there is something terribly out of line, wrong, and harmful in creation as a result of people who pretend they can invent another kind of world. Death is the result of such a willful error, just as it often is the result of drunken driving or careless mountain climbing. There is no alternative to the world God made. Life is now hard but not impossible. Efforts must be made and they will eventually lead to rewarding results. We are called to create families, food, and safety, and rule ourselves through personal virtue and capable community leaders.

The fragility of human intent requires a constant critical mind to evaluate how people and nature exist in relation to the good, just, and loving character of God spoken about by the prophets and apostles and fully lived out in Jesus Christ.

---

28. Levi 19:35ff.

Chapter 9

Work and Effort are your Signature

In Handel's oratorio *Acis and Galatea*, one of the characters sings of love, saying "Without her no Pleasure, for Life is a Pain."[1] This common view, that we are cursed to a painful life of work, is drawn from the biblical statement that the ground we work on is cursed after the rebellion of Adam and Eve. Many people believe that work is for survival and we only find the meaning of life in pleasure. Jacques Ellul, the French sociologist, differentiates between work and calling,[2] seeing work as abnormal and a result of the Fall of Adam, while one's calling is to a higher purpose above whatever work can accomplish. Pieter Bruegel the elder's painting, *Das Schlaraffenland* (1567) portrays a fictitious country where rivers run with milk and honey, and wine instead of water flows from every fountain.[3] Beautifully roasted birds fly through the air, houses are constructed from cake, and the fields abound with stuffed rabbits ready to be eaten and fine cheeses instead of stones. Pleasure is virtuous, work and diligence are sinful.

This dream of idleness is a common response to the hardship of life and work. Solomon adds another note: "I hated all my toil in which I toil under the sun, seeing that I must leave it to the man who will come after me. And who knows whether he will be wise or a fool? Yet he will be master of all for which I have toiled and used my wisdom under the sun."[4]

People engaged in dirty or dangerous work may find these views attractive. In most cultures almost any physical work is considered a

---

1. Georg Friedrich Handel, "Acis and Galatea," with Joan Sutherland, Peter Pears, Owen Brannigan, David Galliver. http://youtube.be/huDR2J95R8ET=4m3s.
2. Jacques Ellul, *Work and Calling*, in Katallegete 4 (Fall/Winter 1972), 8–16.
3. With a hint to Deut 6:3.
4. Eccl 2:18ff.

menial task, a necessity to be eagerly avoided whenever possible. Replacing times for work with festivals and ceremonies is common. The most admired people have others do the necessary work for them. Solomon's lament adds a sense of meaninglessness, recognizing that every effort can so easily be destroyed by the next person or by a cruel exploitive authority in the next generation.

What value is there in work and effort if life itself is vain and without an overarching purpose other than mere survival?

Work makes us dirty, is fraught with danger, and wears us down to an early death. That was certainly the experience of the miners digging for salt in the mountain below my home. Work takes time away from pleasure and other components of human life such as conversation, the arts, and further education. It is understandable that we seek ways to be free from the burden of work, from dirt and pain, and from any kind of necessity.

Humans have long been tempted to use other people in order to avoid unpleasant labor, putting to work those considered to be of a lesser station in life, such as outsiders and even poor neighbors, always in an effort to lighten one's own burden by placing it on the shoulders of others. Europeans and African tribes enslaved strangers from other places, and established immigrants dominated newly arrived people. Indo-Germanic arrivals subjugated the indigenous peasants in South India as Russians also did with people from the Caucasus. The Spanish and Portuguese employed indigenous American Indian populations, and Romans used the people from conquered nations. In Victorian England it was assumed that everyone had been assigned, by God or history, a station in life according to their birth and language. In our own generation we give work to those whom we pay as little as they are willing to accept, without considering how much salary a day's work and a life really require.

In most cultures work is seen as a judgment and curse from the gods. (Many years ago our five-year old daughter informed us that we only had her to do our dishes!) Adopting that view, many "holy people" abstain from worldly occupation, from the market, even from physical dependence on food or sexuality. In the same way intellectuals who work mostly with their mind, look down on those with manual skills: a university degree is considered of greater significance than a certificate of competence in a craft.

The Bible, by presenting God himself as a worker, is our only source for understanding that the purpose of work is more than survival. God imagined every detail of what he subsequently worked to create. He took time to reflect before he formed the diverse objects and living things of the natural world out of original material. He worked the clay of the ground he had made in order to form Adam. God is the "former" in the sense that he is *before* anything else, as one might say, "In former times people had no electric light"; but he is also the "former" in the strict sense that he is the one who gives a form, a shape, to reality, materializing an idea with consequences in the physical world. In Isaiah God speaks of "the work of my hands."[5] Jeremiah contrasts God, who hears and speaks and is in all things wise and wonderful, to idols, who are "stupid and without knowledge." There is no breath in them; they are false images, lifeless delusions skillfully made by goldsmiths. "Not like these is he who is the portion of Jacob, for he is the one who formed all things. Israel is ... his inheritance."[6] God is not a delusion of Israel, and Israel is not a delusion of God; one confirms the other. The human can only be an image of God if there is a God who worked to make him human!

When God's real existence is denied, the possibility of being in the image of God also falls away. All that is left is an impersonal natural universe, which functions but does not in itself explain a purpose. Nature gives only an amoral or value-neutral context for human life. With nature as the only neighborhood, men and women act as biological phenomena performing, at best, arbitrary social roles. The quest for power dictates what is right, and mere appetites direct choices. Fitness determines survival.

When the reality of the image of God is lost, what remains is nature's beast in man.

More Than Just Getting By

Only the Bible proposes that each human person is by definition in God's image, mandated to live and work expressing his or her unique creative personality as well as social responsibility. This adds the extra dimension of "moral duty" to nature's "what is possible." Work is an essential part of being a person—the activity of a creative mind directing skilled hands purposefully each moment the flow of time and the space around us. It is not a result of the fall of Adam and Eve. Its purpose is not primarily survival, but to express the individuality of people with minds and

---

5. Isaiah 45:11; 29:23; 64:8. People are the clay, God is their potter: "we are all the work of your hand."

6. Jer 10:16.

imagination. Only after the fall, with the break-up of what was once a harmonious world, does work become sweaty, more difficult, and often dirty and dangerous as well.

But even after the fall work is not first a matter of necessity, of survival.[7] Instead, it continues to express the significant identity of a choice maker, to mark and single out time and place, to create ownership, and to express personality, inventiveness, and generosity. Through work we resist boredom, evil, hunger, anarchy, death, and all other threats. With it we change nature into culture, random occurrence into lawful order, and manifest power into respected ownership.

What most people associate with work—dirt, sweat, tiredness, or repetition—does not give the activity its identity. Sweat and dirt can be washed off. With sleep we recover our strength for another day. Through effort we gain greater skill and distinct accomplishments. "He who seeks shall surely find" is a general principle about life, not solely a religious promise in the Bible. Diligent workers will find greater satisfaction, fulfillment, and a far more active mind than people caught in routines or following someone else's orders. They have to consider options, search for markets, calculate prices, select and often create their own tools. They figure things out, often on the spur of the moment, in unusual situations and faced with diverse human dilemmas, while so many clerks are paid for not much independent thinking, with no immediate interest in the particular human situation they address. Where they are in a bureaucratic position they have little personal responsibility beyond performing what regulations prescribe. They execute the decisions of distant authorities. Ever act and decision is prescribed by law and implemented without variance. More compliant, cheaper workers can easily replace them.

According to the Bible God intended our work to be rewarded with protected property.[8] over which the person can dispose. Nothing exists that is not made by someone who first has an idea[9] and then brings it into existence in the external world. A hired man is worthy of his pay[10] and you shall not muzzle the mouth of the ox that treads your grain,[11] so that he can eat the reward of his work. Earning wages and acquiring

---

7. Matt 7:7; Luke 11:9; 1 Chron 28:9; 2 Chron 15:2.
8. Exod 20:15.
9. That is the nature of intellectual property.
10. Deut 24:14.
11. Deut 25:4; 1 Cor 9:9; 1 Tim 5:18.

property[12] serve as security and is a source of generous engagement in a compassionate community against this unfair world, where justice is not fully established.[13]

Where this relationship between effort and reward is not respected, for instance in tribal or village societies with communal ownership, or ideological communities advocated by Marxist socialism, the purpose of work is too abstract and soon lost, motivation dwindles, and responsibility becomes undefined and inconsequential. The saying "we pretend to work and they pretend to pay us" aptly describes such a social arrangement. Why make an effort when the outcome is subject to irrational religious powers, unpredictable political schemes, and various forms of corruption? If the benefit or payment for work is reduced to an indefinable and unquantifiable social value, human creativity and productivity are denied, "the image of God" is obscured, and the results for people, their culture, and their economy are tragic.

Contrast that with the Bible's proposition that work is an essential human activity because of the way we are made. We work with our minds and hands. We work to discover, alter, and mark the world. We turn a house into a home; sexual attraction into love, commitment, and service; words into meaningful communication; a piece of land into a source of food and artistic pleasure; sound into songs and symphonies; and all kinds of materials into tools to extend our reach and give shape to our world. Machinery, tools, and musical instruments are extensions of our hands and minds.

Such work is not demeaning but uplifting. The foremost needs of workers are the protection of the law and the honest wages due them, not rest and release from labor.[14] Of course, in an imperfect, fallen and painful world some work is not desirable, but necessary. Not every task is directly fulfilling.[15] But even when the reward is not in the form of pleasure or remuneration, it can still be found in satisfaction and contentment with an achieved goal. There is no unimportant work, for everyone

---

12. Property must not be stolen through theft, inflation, spoilage, deceit, poor quality or in other ways that diminish value.

13. Acts 2:42ff; 4:32; 5:1ff; 6:1–4.

14. James 5:3ff.

15. Some tasks need to be done before other, more fulfilling activities are possible. A soldier needs to protect the area within which love, commerce, and learning can take place. Toilets need cleaning to reduce the threat to life itself by human waste and harmful bacteria.

depends on all the threads of the social fabric holding together, including the careful application of laws by what should not be dismissively labeled bureaucracy.

No type of work can detract from a person's meaningful life, personal value, or image, because each individual already exists prior to any accomplishment and is always significant.

What I think and achieve is evidence of my personality and creates a new situation with real consequences. The idle have few ways to show their significance, their identity. They are not intelligently or morally engaged with anything beyond their space and time. They appear wasted, useless, and replaceable or redundant when nothing and no one depends on them.

People At Work

In the garden of Eden, Adam studied the world around him and loved Eve. He talked with God and explored the satisfaction that comes from dominion. When the fall made life more problematic and survival was threatened by a surrounding nature that became hostile, he tilled the land and gave thistles their limits. Later, Abraham and Isaac dug wells to irrigate the land for the richer pastures their growing herds needed.[16]

The Bible tells of shepherds and prophets, artisans, poets and musicians. Miners look for iron and copper under every hill.[17] There are kings and fishermen, women baking, and lawyers and judges administering justice in city gates to protect the innocent. Sailors set out to sea and traders give Jonah a ride on their ship. Carpenters build houses, the King's palace, and the Lord's Temple. Paul makes tents; judges administered justice in city gates and protected the innocent. Soldiers secure the land and tax collectors ensure that everyone shares the common burden. Priests serve the public by strengthening their relationship to a known God. Government prevents evil and furthers what is good for everyone.[18]

People at work are the background of the biblical record. People at work are illustrations for many of Jesus' parables. The Bible gives us many accounts of God's work through human agency, whether farmers who sow their seeds and collect the harvest, or judges who listen to God's law and adjudicate it to correct errors and punish evildoers. Others skillfully

16. Gen 26.
17. Deut 8:3ff.
18. Rom 13:1–7.

repair walls, bridges, and waterways. Couples marry and have children for the benefit of the whole human race. Doctors mend bones and fight attacks on the body, including bacteria, viruses, and cancer. They intervene to keep a person alive, able to see, think and understand, to enjoy beauty, the presence and kindness of others, and the attention of their family. They even amputate a limb or transplant an organ to allow a person's mind, soul, and heart to continue with as rich a life as possible.

All work is an expression that we are human beings rather than part of an impersonal natural program; we live in a world shaped by our thoughts and values, a world of purposes pursued, of justice and fairness sought and at times achieved as God originally intended. While the natural world functions well as a closed system, human participation opens it to the wonder of additional experiences, products, and a host of aesthetic variations and moral improvements.

The ideal life is not idleness, rest, or retirement, but significant and rewarded activity in every domain of human abilities, so that everyone will be able to eat from the vine he has tended and the fig tree he harvests. That is the spiritual activity, rightly understood, of each of us, involving our hands and minds, our heart and soul, our declared intentions, and our desire for life in tune with what God's Spirit has told us in the Bible.

Spirituality is not a higher calling or an abdication of material work, intellectual discernment, and physical activity. The Bible shows that God's work intimately involves space/time material realities. Since life is threatened by injustice, cruelty, and death, our work has the additional purpose of opposing evil. There is no higher calling than to protect life, seek justice, and resist all forms of evil. It is spiritual in the sense that God's Spirit informs us that work in the search for justice is good. In the Bible there is no spiritual focus without material, historical ramifications. Our goal is not to go to heaven, liberated from necessary effort now, but to prepare for the return of Christ on earth and then an ongoing life without the complications of the fall.

God's creation, for himself as well as for us, is a real world in a real universe, a space/time reality where all human life takes place. Death is an enemy,[19] not an escape from physical bodies, even though they may not function well now, do not always get the food and drink they need, and can be wounded and die. The burden we carry is not our bodies, but death manifested in our bodies. We should not seek to be free from our

---

19. 1 Cor 15:26.

bodies, but work to make them healthier, to use them well, and see them as part of who we are in the image of God.

The Bible says death breaks up the psychophysical unit of body and soul, making life temporarily impossible for a whole person who would otherwise invent and produce, compose and perform, and love and serve. We do not *have* a body, we *are* a body and soul, and as such are persons, living creatures by force of God's breath of life.[20] Man and woman are biological beings in a relationship to God that is only possible between persons.

For that reason we fight against death, whether early in life or later on. All along life's trajectory we work with our hands and minds, we create fields and homes, sow seeds and harvest grains and fruit. We fish at sea and weave cloth for our clothes. We make life more possible with the help of laws to protect us against evil people. We study how the body works, how food is digested, how muscles are maintained and how much we need to drink to flush out the waste after our bodies have used the nutrients from the food we eat.

We build dams and dig wells; we learn what animals are helpful to our needs and which are harmful to our crops. We dress ourselves for warmth, protection, and privacy. We read and write in order to have more access to what people say, to pose questions and offer advice, and to learn from others. We do math in order to calculate measurements and angles, as well as to pay no more than an object is worth and figure out what remains for other things.

All work, whether practical, aesthetic, or philosophical, involves the whole person.

We work, love, and search for wisdom and the justice people deserve because of their dignity as human beings made in God's image. Among Christians that effort is also born from the expectation of the coming of the Messiah, the return of Jesus in history. The Bible promises that he will one day restore what human life was meant to be all along, and rule on earth with power and justice. Believing God and trusting his Holy Spirit are not the expression of irrational feelings and otherworldly concerns; rather, they are the true basis for living well and right with appreciation for creation. Sorrow runs deep over all that is wrong in creation and between people now, including the curse of each deplorable death, but we also look forward to new life when creation is repaired.

---

20. Gen 2:7.

Chapter 10

Laws to Restrain Evil

FROM EVERYTHING WE HAVE considered so far, we know that the universe functions regularly and lawfully in its natural processes without contradictions. We are familiar with an orderly world, not a random one. Without God or man, reality would just function. It is what it is. But as soon as moral personality is included, this rational world becomes unfair and contains contradictions and injustice. With the notion of a moral god and the moral judgments made by every person throughout history, objections arise for which only the Bible gives an intellectual answer: there has been a break with what was once good but is no longer.

This world is enriched by a multitude of creatively good choices but impoverished through sinful and bad choices. There are choices by God, who can appoint a king and punish a bad one, feed 5000 people miraculously,[1] and even make a donkey talk when that is the only way for a man to listen to what God has to say.[2] Through human choices we have both benefits and losses; we are better off because of the good work of people, and worse off because of failures, deliberate evil, and hatred. That is why our orderly world is not completely good and acceptable. Poison, human greed, and other manifestations of a damaged world and human sin surround us. Both good and evil choices start their own secondary but always orderly process of consequences, some good and many clearly bad. Even though there is nothing random about the world (there is no luck or chance in the sense of effects without a cause or a cause without an effect), it is still imperfect and marred by the pursuit of

1. John 6:1ff.
2. Num 22:21ff.

false ideas and their logical consequences brought about with scientific rationality and steady logic.

This world of real personages who are able and even mandated to make choices out of their own deliberation or free will has been damaged and is now filled with problems because of poor choices in the past that produce painful and destructive consequences. Additional unfairness results when the consequences affect not only the choice-maker's life but continue into the lives of others, innocent bystanders, and future generations. The person making the first choice is alone responsible, but all the others who follow suffer the consequences. They suffer from being next in line in history, not through any fault of their own. The time when each person will only be exposed to the consequences of his or her own choices is not yet here.[3] Such is the reality of our significance and the effect of our actions and choices, including the choice not to act and to merely let things be.

For that reason a culture informed by the Bible's view of life identifies people, whether inventors, criminals, poets, or thieves, by their names. Praise or blame is due to those who start a chain of events with practical intellectual, economic, and social-political results.

We have seen that the Bible is very realistic about unfairness when problems we face and burdens we carry are the result of someone else's choices. A mother who does not eat well gives birth to a sickly child. If a father is idle and gets drunk, the whole family suffers. A man is handicapped with blindness because he inherits the long term consequences of Adam's foolish choice to disobey God.[4] A business owner may use bad materials, make his workers sick, lose customers, and eventually ruin his enterprise. Someone else takes advantage of unemployed people, hiring them at a wage inadequate for their needs, while still earning a high income for himself from their labor. Some take advantage of the ignorance of others to sell them things they do not need, or items of inferior quality that easily break. Why do the wicked frequently prosper and the righteous so often suffer?[5]

---

3. Ezek 18.

4 Jesus refutes the suggestion that a handicap is the result of personal guilt: John 9:1–34. The blind man was the innocent victim of someone else's sin all the way back to Adam and Eve. The term sin in John's Gospel in most instances describes the reality of imperfection.

5. Ps 73:3, 12.

Laws to Restrain Evil

Frequent biblical references to God's initially good world, created true to his wishes and character, support the human quest to understand and benefit from it. Creation was good, the work of a steadfast person who remains always true to himself in everything he has done and promises to do in the future. The orderliness of creation is the design and purpose of an orderly person. The messiness of creation or nature, and unfair experiences of life, including unmerited failure or success, are the result of human creative intervention. The world is today no longer good and just. However, we are freed from its poor model, which no longer reflects the moral character of a creator, to create a better human society.

For that reason many people throughout history have found that God's law provides a clear moral approach to reality, a way to exercise dominion over both the physical world and flawed human ideologies. This is clarified in the text of the Bible and the person of Jesus through instructions that free us from the cues of nature's laws by imposing moral law on nature, including human nature. We are no longer imbedded in nature, but belong to a distinct group or species, those "in the image of God." Instead of being copycats of impersonal nature and its suffering victims, we can exercise dominion to make careful use of it.

In order to do well *and* be good, to please God and neighbor, and to work with a clear conscience using the materials of the physical world, as well as what we think and say, we must correct our outlook on life away from what nature does and circumstances allow. In a moral universe we are under the person of God and his judgment. Our choices matter, and their consequences will be weighed and measured by God, our neighbors, our children, and future generations.

Much of what we understand of life comes with our understanding that Nature tells us what is possible and impossible, while God tells us what is moral, good, and right. Nature has rules of behavior built into its structures. A stone will always behave like a stone, a cow like a cow, a river like water running downhill.

What is natural for people is very different. Making choices is a central part of being human. We require practical skills to choose between factual options, but only moral judgment directs our choice between moral options. The choice we should make is not built into us, for we are created to originate choices and live by our creativity. We don't do what we ought to do by nature alone or naturally. To make right choices we need a moral orientation, not what is simply possible or convenient in the family, in society, or in business. Respect for the lawfulness of creation removes fear from human existence because it is tied to the lawfulness of God's eternal being. He is both powerful and morally just. From God we learn what is good for the moral order to function well, as individuals and as a society.

The Bible introduces us to a God who is not an impersonal force or a moody power, though we might expect moody actions from human beings. God has a character, faithful and defined, is reliable, and has a distinct way of thinking and doing. God is not everything, nor in everything, nor doing everything. In fact, his justice limits and defines his power to do only good. The Bible refers to that as the holiness of God, and we are called to be holy as well.[6] The God of the Bible is always good, loving, just, and compassionate. He is distinct, a specific person with a particular will and purpose. That is why there is a created, definite reality, in which things are distinguished rather than muddled. God is bound to be himself, unable to contradict who he is or what he has said, done, and promised. This is the God of the Bible who tells us what is right, beneficial, and appropriate for us.

Orderly Nature, But Commands for Good

To survive we must discover, respect, obey, and apply the laws of nature. But nature does not tell us what is good; it contains both harm and harmony. To do good and prevent harm, to value our significance and live rightly before God and neighbors, we must also discover, respect, obey, and apply his commands.

We have seen that God is a worker; he thought and created, accomplishing what he set out to do, and was pleased. His work benefited everything he created and made life possible, though its continuity was dependent on a contract of obedience between God and Adam and Eve. God would be faithful, supportive, and provide instructions and explanations. Adam and Eve were given assignments to have dominion, to work in the garden, to be fruitful and multiply. Through their work they would expand the possibilities of God's world, benefit from its promise, and serve him by continuing to shape and arrange what he had made. God did not make a place for play, but rather for the discovery and pleasure of fulfilling and rewarding work. The development of mental and manual

---

6. Exod 19:6, "You shall be a holy nation"; Lev 20:7, "You shall be holy!"; Heb 12:10, "That we may share in his holiness."

skills would be a satisfying reward, as would the discovery of more and diverse ways to affect the external world by making significant choices. The first people were invited to discover and find satisfaction and pleasure in the inexhaustible variety of ways to be human.

Our Continuously Weighty Significance

The proposition that all human beings are made in God's image encourages us to work purposefully as part of the moral order in a world where everything is "according to the kind" it was created to be. As I pointed out earlier, under the influence of the Bible work is no longer considered a curse, an interruption of free time, a painful seriousness that interferes with our desire to play and live an idle existence. Together with thought and speech, work is one of the central means we have to express our existence as unique persons. It affects the context for each life and consequently is different for each of us who strive to make life more pleasant, safe, and nourishing for everybody.

Through people tools are made, food is cultivated, governments are established, and life is artistically embellished. People also discern problems in nature, and seek to understand death in all its many forms and appearances. They develop means to combat, solve, and at times remove these problems, which can at least be identified and singled out with a name, a label, for future solutions. That already is a success, for then events no longer happen unobserved, but are appraised by us as moral agents. In our thoughts and with our words we oppose evil and promote good.

We work not only for ourselves, but we also lay the groundwork for the next generation. Each generation stands on the shoulders of what others have accomplished, for both good and ill. Either we start out with the benefits of what was gained, or have to catch up and repair what others before us lost or neglected. Everyone's life is significant, with consequences for all history.

Furthermore, we work for a surplus, for more than the amount needed for immediate survival, because we treasure life and want to make it as colorful, diverse, and encouraging as possible. In the Bible people were to work for more than their daily needs. They worked six days and lived seven, including the day of rest from the burden of life in a fallen, problematic world. They also worked to nourish and provide for their young children and those too old to harvest their own fields or earn their support. They worked even more, because of what they gave in charity and in taxes, or tithes, so that the landless priests, lawyers and teachers, the poor and sick, the handicapped, and the city administrators would all be paid in kind or from market profits. Jesus said that Caesar should have what he needs for his work, but to God we owe our hearts and minds, including the whole world of our ideas.[7] Caesar's face was on the coins, but God's image is on our whole being.

Carefully observing a fallen world should awaken further reasons to work for more than our immediate needs. Lean years can follow fat ones,[8] and unforeseeable emergencies can arise. We need to reduce loss due to spoilage, waste, and natural enemies like mice, rats, and other pests. "Be fruitful!" contains, beyond the call to have children, the idea to do better than before, to expand options, learn from mistakes, and improve the human situation at all times. It encompasses the drive to improve products and invent new ones out of a desire to make life safer, more colorful, and less wasteful. Artists sign their work to own and mark their limited influence in a life time and as a statement against oblivion; for, even though it may have no immediate practical benefit, their work does state that a human being has put his or her mark on a slice of reality.

Each person also contributes to the workings of government "by consent of the governed." Consent is an active participation for good rule, public justice, and a civil society rather than silent acceptance or resigned indifference. Like a child applying what it received from parents in order to build and improve on it, we should not get stuck in the repetition of the past, but look ahead. What we accomplish now with knowledge and wisdom, expressed in practical efforts and lively debates, is the only way we can be assured that we are real persons, not lost or destroyed, for our works shall follow after.[9]

Honest Commitments

Beyond moral concerns, work itself demands honesty, truth, and trustworthiness, when you want your efforts and accomplishments to create a good reputation as part of your good and virtuous life. Your

---

7. Matt 22:21.
8. Gen 41:22–57.
9. Rev 14:13.

neighbors, your community and descendents, and your own reputation all depend on them.

You will recall that God's moral laws do not impose restrictions, but are always rooted in the nature of reality as it is constructed, where things and processes function in a specific and orderly way, "according to their kind." Honesty in the material world should be reflected in the honesty of personal and professional work to improve the local situation and meet real needs. There should be no deception or confusion between the appearance of something and its true quality. As words must not deceive, neither should weights and measures give a false impression, like the facades of "Potemkin villages"[10] that deceptively impress with the appearance of reality but cannot house people or last through the winter.

Jesus tells us that our "yes" should really mean "yes," that there should be a correspondence between what something is and what is said about it, how it is presented. The only moral way to make use of materials, people, and machines and all things is to be honest in relation to what they are.

As always, such obligations are tied to what God created: real things, real time and space, precise definitions. Anything that does not reflect those characteristics is deceitful and dishonest, as it presents a vain appearance rather than the substance of things. The true nature of reality is the bottom line for all factual, moral, and relational or contractual considerations. There is no way forward, no solution for the hardships, without being profoundly and genuinely concerned with truth, fact, and substance, whether in matters of faith and belief, or in our daily work.

In other words, the pursuit of a virtuous life should come from a choice to conform to the way God, people, and creation show order, honesty, and truth. Honesty and diligence reflect factual realizations rather than personal values, demonstrating that materials I work with have a nature, a definition, and particular characteristics which I respect in my work. I value similar characteristics in myself, for I do not want to be known as untrustworthy, a shoddy laborer, a deceitful fly-by-night handyman, the subject of gossip and accusations. Furthermore, because I believe what the Bible tells me about God and history, I strive for honesty and other virtues from a desire to please God and contribute to what is right, rather than allowing opportunity to dictate my behavior. I want

---

10. A term used to describe the use by Gregori Potemkin of an impressive façade to hide an undesirable or damaged condition of fake villages along the road his empress Catherine the Great of Russia was to travel.

to be in charge, not driven by appetites and short-term goals to make a deceptive temporary impression until the truth is revealed.

The contract of exchanging work for payment is an area in which substance is more important than appearance. In order to serve the people we employ we owe them their wages when they are due. Scripture and common sense tell us that wages must not be withheld overnight, neither a man's coat[11] nor the means of production, nor may the poverty of a widow be used to justify taking a pledge from her.[12] These actual obligations from the contractual nature of employment limit the power of the employer over the employee. Just wages are set by what is due, not by what any person can get away with or make excuses for.

The employer's responsibility is to provide a safe and clean work space and a fair wage to sustain life for the employee's immediate family. That life consists of more than survival for another day's work and must include time for family relationship, the enjoyment of each member with others and ways to genuinely rest each night and day. Wages must be paid in a timely manner for the gain realized by the employee's work. An employer respects his employee by providing an honest description of the work and its context. That is a part of caring for a person, a neighbor to be loved as one loves and cares for oneself. What is the purpose of the product, where does it fit into the larger pursuits of the company, why does it matter that the work is executed carefully and precisely? What training is included to satisfy the employee's need for personal development? Where a person is employed instead of a machine, an explanation stimulates his or her logical reasoning and gives the insight needed to understand both the job and its contribution to the larger world. That is the only honorable thing to do; explanations train people to think, to make better decisions, and to take initiative in process improvements.

Employees also have obligations towards their employer under the same contract. They are responsible to be punctual, healthy, and diligent as part of a disciplined approach to life, a way of working that corresponds to the laws that govern time, ability, and integrity. Without taking proper care of hygiene one gets sick more easily and becomes unreliable. Lack of punctuality wastes time and energy, leads to unnecessary worry, and sows mistrust among everyone in a business.

---

11. Exod 22:26.
12. Deut 24:6–17.

Diligence demonstrates intensity and focus on accomplishment. Diligent people agree with the job description and understand how weighty their contribution is to the task. They are careful also in what they eat and that they sleep enough to maintain their health and the ability to concentrate. They separate work defined by the boss from time outside of work defined by themselves. They do not let others down, but pull their own weight to keep the cart moving and get the work done. While not being married to the job, they remain faithful to contractual commitments and consider how everything they do outside of work may affect their performance. Diligent workers do not bring outside problems to bear on their work commitment. They keep their vows, first to spouse and family, with basic faithfulness as a character trait in all of life. They are loyal and do not betray inside knowledge to outsiders, but also initiate debate and challenge bad decisions out of loyalty to their business and co-workers.

The Bible gives us rich teaching and illustrations of the importance of diligence, which must be distinguished from restless ambition on one side and complacent neglect on the other. We should "not light our own fire and go in its light," and do things more from enthusiasm than insight and skill, for that obviously lacks wisdom.[13] Enthusiasm that lacks wisdom ignores the orderly way the world functions.

On the other hand, there is Jesus' parable of the various talents, in which one person loses all because he is too fearful to invest it.[14] Talents represent purposeful engagement to acquire knowledge and insight for life, pleasure, and satisfaction, and to diminish the pain that is always part of human existence.

The diligent person applies himself to an endeavor, uses his skills, knowledge, wisdom, and time to accomplish his goal in its distinct character and definition. Diligence involves seeing the whole picture rather than a list of individual prescriptions of behavior. It springs from genuine comprehension of what a job requires, what a contract demands. Individual significance lies in the correct execution of a task for the benefit of others. Diligence is an expression of love for the work that needs to be done and for the people you value. You give your full attention to pursue the assigned task in a steady effort because you understand that, alongside your personal satisfaction from a task well done, other people are served and a foundation laid for the inheritance of future generations.

13. Isa 50:11.
14. Matt 25:14ff.

God and Man at Work

It is not surprising that the diligence demanded by a job is again related to the shape of God's creation. Creation provides a larger framework in which we comprehend our calling as faithful human beings. Diligence is a human response to any task in a world which the Bible describes as the work of a diligent creator God. He set to work creating the world in great detail, and it is our mandate to give it a refined shape, more variety and, where necessary, a corrected bend away from the harm that is now regrettably also part of creation.

God worked each day of creation. He discussed, decided, and demonstrated what he had in mind by creating a real history with people as individual bearers of his image. No wonder he was pleased and called good what he set out to accomplish, and no wonder that our word "good" indicates quality, consistency, beauty, and generous benevolence, since its root meaning is derived from the word God.

Under the influence of Hegel's view of dialectic history, conflict, competition, oppression, and exploitation are seen as the central explosive forces that advance the course of history. Freud suggests that the need to use people for sexual satisfaction is the foundation of all human relations. But that has been just as seriously discredited as the view that history advances through class and gender struggles. Instead of sex, a human being's most central needs are love, respect, and attentive compassion and admiration.[15]

These needs are best addressed in Christianity, which holds that people are not accidents of history, but must carefully contribute to and direct it. Nature, which prepares us poorly for that task and treats people with indifference, should be subject to human dominion for the benefit of all. We also exercise dominion in the way we choose to love our co-workers as neighbors. Training employees to handle more responsibility honors them and allows us to depend on their efforts and growing skills. We love them out of concern for their humanity and to help them fully understand this world and their place in it.

We should endeavor steadfastly to live full human lives, to work with mind and hands, to make use of time and harness available energy toward the goal of solving real problems. Our true work is to change the world, including ourselves, so that it contains less of what sin and the subsequent fall brought and more of what God originally intended.

---

15. Willard Gaylin's *Rediscovering Love* (Penguin, 1987) describes this from the insight of a post-Freudian psychoanalyst.

We choose to love because we know the other person is a human being rather than a machine or a bundle of biological influences. We stand up, create good, and resist evil, rather than lie low and merge with the impersonal world. Diligence will have consequences, for we know that reality is not random, but subject to cause and effect. Work brings its rewards, for significant actions always produce results in both the intellectual/spiritual realm and the external world. There is a crown to be earned and a name to be recorded before mankind and God for our accomplishments in history.

Chapter 11

Signposts for the Open Range

IN CHAPTER SEVEN WE noted that the Bible's prescriptions and rules are not arbitrary statements of willful power. They are not religious in nature, nor are they rules for membership in a club or church. Their purpose is not to check whether we would be willing to obey. God does not use his position as creator to demand submission to senseless rules. Some parents impose their will on their children, bosses on their employees, and of course rulers on their subjects. The Bible and God's commandments can be taught in this way, but this is a misplaced focus on obedience rather than on appreciative comprehension.

In most religions, in some businesses, and in many families individuals are expected to be silent and obedient and compliant to create the illusion of tidy conformity and predictability. The authority, the boss, or the spiritual ruler determines what keeps everyone in line to give an impression that all is in order, true, and permanent. The individual husband, wife, child, employee, or true believer no longer has to think. Being told what to believe, what to do, and what to repeat, creates a sense of security so that there is no reason to ask any questions or raise any doubts.

However, such an authoritarian structure creates a profound problem: nothing is ever examined, improved, or advanced. There is no room for review, for reconsidering teachings and practices. Neither a past and present failure, nor the vivid imagination of alternatives, is allowed in a search for new ideas. Centrally controlled economies apply this method, as do many family structures and state-run businesses. In each case quasi-religious dictates about everything from product selection to pricing, about the defined roles of men, women, and children, etc. are assumed to be the final word. Such a method instills order but shows little concern for truth and the need to adjust to diverse and often changing situations.

The point of God's commands is the opposite. Rather than demanding conformity at all times, they focus our priority on the pursuit of truth, to show compassion for human beings, and seek justice in a complex and troubled world. The prohibitive commands outline the pitfalls we are warned against to prevent damage through ignorance or neglect. The truth is that God created the world with a specific shape and definition, regardless of one's personal opinion, religion, or political orientation. It is not up to us to invent it, for the real world exists already.

Of course, the ability to invent things is part of being a person. We are free to invent within the possibilities and limitations of the original definitions and will benefit from it. We can, for instance, invent different ways to store water for later use or to purify it for reuse after it has been polluted. But we cannot make a world in which water is lighter than air, where it can flow uphill, or where drinking dirty water is harmless. Neither are we able to invent a different way to be born than how it was established from the start through one father and one mother.

In business there is no better way to improve products, participate in the market, make a profit for everyone, and select what should be made and sold, than to let competence be sharpened through competition. That presents a constant challenge as we review what we already have and search for something better, more efficient, less costly, and with fewer side effects.

What each person does in any family and how they all contribute to the functioning of this smallest social unit is different, regardless of the gender of each member. The Bible's emphasis on one common human race, and on the equality of male and female persons, has led to productive, humane arrangements of respectful interplay and mutual help, where the only real difference is the gender of father and mother. Any additional limit on freedom and individuality disregards the mind, the inventiveness, and the intellectual workings and uniqueness of each person. The facts of nature, such as children being carried for nine months by the mother, are universally binding. Beyond such a biological and material definition, everything is universally liberating which encourages discoveries, release of creative energy, and personal enjoyment.

Each person's unique ability to think, evaluate, decide, and contribute must have room to express itself. Many women can do some work better than men, and often children are more perceptive and more thoughtful in certain important areas than their parents. There is no fixed role for male and female in Scripture, no limit that one or the other must do a specific job in the family, beyond what each chooses to do by an act of the will first, and then according to their physical abilities and time constraints.

Scripture pays great respect to this equality, often teaching in verse couplets because no single sentence can fully describe the complexity of a relationship. For example, husbands are to leave father and mother and cleave to their wives,[1] but wives should submit to their husbands;[2] yet again husbands should serve their wives the way Christ serves the church.[3] Children ought to obey their parents, but parents in turn must not drive their children to anger.[4]

Introduction to the Work Place

Biblical commands do not add to what already exists or create new obligations, but attempt to remind us of what is already part of the workings and shape of the real world. In them the creator lays out the kind of world he made, our relationship to it, and how we can live within its boundary conditions without getting hurt at every turn. His purpose is not to establish a religious association but aid us in discovering how reality is constituted and how it should function. He instructs us, as a users' guide does for a new appliance, concerning the basics for human relationships, so that we can live in this world with its specific form.

There are then reasons for God's commands, which we should critically consider, discuss, and understand. One would expect a continuous rational link between the personality of an author, his creation, and his description of it for the curious. A reasonable God would make a reasonable creation where everything has a distinct explanation and where there is no confusion between what is real and imaginary, what is good and evil, what is life and death. We can trust and affirm God's reasonable being because of the evidence that he knows what he is talking about, is faithful to himself and without contradiction, mood swings, or arbitrary acts of a changing will. In all eternity evil will never be a part of good and no death part of what God had planned for life. The biblical record

1. Gen 2:24.
2. Eph 5:22.
3. Eph 5:25ff.
4. Col 3:20–21.

states that God binds himself to his promises, to his decision to create the world, and to love people made in his image. He cannot will otherwise. Those aspects of God's character are non-negotiable and make the description of "good" sensible. They are not randomly chosen, selectively applied, or arbitrarily expressed. They describe his Being, a Tri-unity of Persons who love one another. Love, faithfulness, mercy, and grace are not additions to God's basic character which could be lost or abandoned, not occasional or random expressions of his existence; they are intrinsic to his nature. Without these God would not be God.

It is interesting that gods in other religions are not so bound. Either they have no fixed character and do both good and evil because they are one among many competing and performing deities; or, if a unitary, single god with a will, he has no limiting attributes and can consequently do as he pleases, both good and evil. People following these ideas of a god do not find the confidence and assurance needed for a purposeful direction in their life, work, and social arrangements.

The God of the Bible is bound to love, to be full of grace and compassion at all times, not by choice only, but by his nature and as an expression of his character. God is unable to lie[5] or be unloving.

Necessary Instructions

There are always reasons behind God's commandments that we may uncover. There must be a sense to them, a benefit to us in understanding how they structure life. These rules and regulations describe the world God made in the first place, so when we violate them we are not punished by God as an act of his authoritative power, but simply as the consequence of contradicting the workings of the world. God does not have to act directly, for punishment comes swiftly when reality responds to our neglect of its form and function. A lie is not the truth; a false view about poisonous mushrooms, whether from ignorance or arrogance, will lead to the death of all who eat them, regardless of their intentions.

Therefore, the biblical commandments are not arbitrary moral prescriptions, something the boss requires. Beyond simple obedience, they provide a fundamental understanding of the shape of creation, for all moral prescriptions are evident in God's created world.

---

5. Heb 6:18.

That understanding has been a great help to many. We need to know what wrongs the laws should prevent, what good behavior needs no law, and why laws prescribe a certain set of choices to prevent evil or a poorly functioning society. We always need an explanation. Our questions not only ask "what" in any area, they are also ask "why." The Bible always gives a direct explanation when one is not clear from the larger context, so that when we comprehend what is required, what must be obeyed, and what ought to be believed, it is easier to comply.

A remaining problem involves the will; submission is difficult because of the war within us between what we know to be right and what we actually choose to do. We are damaged, as Paul describes so well in his letter to the church at Rome.[6] There is a deep conflict in each of us between what we know to be good and what we wish to do.

The following considerations will help us reduce the power of that conflict, and our reflective humanity will become more evident as we make choices based on understanding rather than emotion, fear of guilt, or blind responses.

The ability of Scripture to give explanations helps us decide to believe God and be thankful for Jesus Christ. When good reasons and satisfactory explanations are not provided, religions and ideologies can too easily demand and then exploit obedience and trust. A fallen world is too confusing, dangerous, and untidy to obey someone without prior inquiry, and to believe without examining the worthiness of a claim. Around the world human history has been terribly damaged by people all too ready to obey false authorities and believe empty claims, imagined gods, and other charlatans who manufacture titles, power structures, and arrogant claims of superior knowledge and far-out myths.

Previously we looked at reasons undergirding some of the Ten Commandments.[7] The same reasonable basis can be seen for the religious and sanitary laws given to the Jewish people.[8] Their central purpose is to make people conscious and decisive concerning matters of daily life. They remind everyone to be responsible, to weigh arguments and situations carefully before distinguishing between what is good and right, what is bad and wrong. In a world of facts we must not embrace a fantasy. In a world of life and death, we must choose life. In a world with deceit

---

6. Rom 7:7–25.

7. See the end of chapter seven, page 104.

8. E.g. the law against cooking the kid in its mother's milk is a reminder that life and death form a drastic contrast.

and error we must hold our own moral ground. Danger is everywhere; we must at all times consider how to live wisely, whom to trust, and even where to sleep. All choices in daily life require careful deliberation. Since no choice is without consequences we should consider what is right and good before we become responsible for what follows. At every moment during our lifetime we need to figure out how to decide for good and against evil, deceit, and finally death.

This also applies to the structures and ethics of human relations, including the kind relationships necessary for a business to function well. Here we need more encompassing insight than what is needed to govern a religious organization in order to speak to all human relations in the family, in business, and in society.

Holiness As Wholeness

The Bible sums up all concerns and obligations for human society with the reminder that we should be holy as God is holy. Holiness is not found in a mental or spiritual focus on another world, but on the continuity between knowledge and action, on a moral life of integrity. It relates to what is solid, reliable, and coherent in our outlook and practice of life in contrast to what is undefined, arbitrary, and irrationally disjointed; to principle rather than circumstance; deciding to pursue a deliberate effort, not each irresponsible and random opportunity; and making sensible decisions instead of responding to passing appetites. In a moral wilderness of largely unprincipled people the life of the Christian should be marked by what is personal holiness in the form and manner I suggest.

Leviticus, the third book of Moses, addresses many issues of holiness in the life of a nation, an organization of neighbors with a common designation as a people. It begins with the double obligation to respect father and mother and to observe the Sabbath.[9] The curious combination of human relations and Sabbath observance makes a foundational assertion. It establishes an understanding of the unique place of persons to each of us and to God. We honor father and mother because we are born in a family line, and we keep the Sabbath to recognize that people are like God and unlike everything else in nature, distinct from animals, plants, and things, which never take a day off. Knowing that the first human

---

9. Lev 19:3.

death was a fratricide,[10] we must maintain a high regard for the life of our brothers (and sisters) and focus on their needs. They are the crown of God's creation. In them, rather than in natural things or animals, is the most distinct evidence for the personal being of God.

We are next told to be generous to the poor, to leave some fruit and grain behind after harvest, and not to squeeze the last drop out of every opportunity. Failing to do this by greedily gathering every last bit of the harvest is a form of theft that deceives and defrauds our neighbors,[11] because we owe them generosity, kindness, and compassion. We are all in this experience of life together, and for some it is more unfair than for others. Neither circumstances nor the market make moral decisions, only people can do that.

Similarly we show respect and diminish the tragic reality of human life in a fallen world by paying a person when the wages are due,[12] and not cursing or laughing at the misfortune of others.[13] We need to deal justly with each situation; justice is not a matter of law, power, or rule, but of ad-justing, or straightening out, all things fairly and truthfully.[14]

Life is unfair, problems are not always of our own making, and illness is rarely the result of personal neglect or sin. In other words, we can not assume that everyone deserves what he or she experiences, whether for good or evil, whether in sickness or in health. What happens in real life is not always right before God, or planned or willed by him. Therefore, we also must do justice to a person's situation and not assume that it is deserved, just and merited. Justice is a matter of weighing and judging what contributes to a given situation, which may well include undeserved factors in the larger circle of people's lives such as their family, birth, and health, or the geography and weather of their home area. Much of Scripture reminds us of the unfairness of life and establishes our obligation to remember the poor[15] precisely because life is hard and unjust.

---

10. Gen 4:8.
11. Lev 19:9–13.
12. Lev 19:13.
13. Lev 19:14.
14. Lev 19:15–18.
15. Gal 2:10; Heb 13:16; Acts 11:29ff, 24:17; Rom 15:25–28, 31; 1 Cor 16:1–4, 15.

Wholeness in All of Life

Holiness requires that we obey God's instructions and decrees by keeping in mind that their purpose is to direct us in a creative and carefully considered life of moral choices. Power, politics, and position in society do not determine what is good and just. To remind us of the importance of such discernment chapter 19 of Leviticus presents three settings in which it can be neglected or become impossible: mating different kinds of animals, planting a field with two kinds of seeds, and wearing clothes made of two different materials.[16] The point is that the same kinds of animals have to mate for young ones to be conceived and born; only one kind of seed should be sown in a field if a harvest to be easy and without frustration. You wouldn't want to sow a second kind of seed in the same field; and two kinds of materials should not be woven together into one cloth to avoid producing ugly and disfigured garments that wash, dry, and shrink differently.

God's laws and rules clearly relate to the rational, defined universe he created. They help us know what is true, good, and right in a life of work and trade; they improve the spiritual and material environment of human beings instead of making life more difficult with religious rituals which always interrupt the focus on a good life. The God of the Bible created and affirms life in all its colors. He does not distract us by imposing time consuming and mind dulling religious fervor or restrictions that diminish the heart of what he intended when he made us in his image.

God's attitude to human life is demonstrated in his original command to subdue the earth. One can subdue by exercising power, by simply exploiting the earth. But much more is implied by the term: to subdue something is to impose a shape and purpose on it, to master its usefulness by making of it something new, whether bricks for housing, shovels for field work, or scrap iron for tools. We, both male and female, thoughtfully use our minds to find and shape the earth's resources and enjoy their usefulness. Everything God created is good and nothing should be rejected.[17]

For the same reason that we are called to make things for our enjoyment, we also structure families and businesses, markets, laws and contracts, and courts to watch over their application. Creating these and other organizations and institutions is a unique human ability. Animals

16. Lev 19:19, 6:17.
17. 1Tim 4:3–5.

do not trade their products for other things or for currency as a portable means of exchange. Only people trade for things made by clever minds in other parts of the country or world. Such trade opens and stretches our mind and appetite to alternate ways of making life easier, more beautiful, and more survivable. It also requires trust based on just measures and fair weights,[18] with judges supervising and guaranteeing accuracy to preserve that trust.

Unlike humans, animals do not assign different parts of a project to those best trained to do them. They do not share in work or its benefits. They do not train, improve, and help one another advance to higher responsibilities. By contrast, people are called to live and learn, to be distinct, not a copy of everyone else, mindlessly repeating what has already been done. Skills, intentions, and motivations become personal and individual, and specializations develop from refined abilities. Communities of specialized workers accomplish many kinds of tasks, not always the same few. Freedom and pleasure rather than envy and regret flow from this view of the individuality of each person; for when everything and everyone does not have to be the same, diversity becomes a source of recognition and admiration.

By contrast, diversity is a threat that leads to envy and suspicion in collective societies like the Marxist model or tribal groups; it must be destroyed because it challenges their monolithic or egalitarian assumptions.

Contractual arrangements and promised commitments between skillful people reflect how God made covenants or contracts with his people. They must value relationships with others on many personal, professional, and intellectual levels, and solidify them through binding agreements with mutual respect and admiration for the work the other person as a supplier can accomplish better. Honoring the different abilities God has given to each person[19] instead of taking advantage of them benefits everyone.[20]

In his letter to the church in Ephesus Paul describes God's generosity, his expressed purposes, and his use of human beings to accomplish things. God's gifts are not arbitrary handouts without the individual person's choice and effort. All people have gifts, abilities and ways to express their unique personhood. That is how God made us, unlike animals,

---

18. Lev 19:35ff; Deut 25:13–16; Jer 32:25, 42–44.
19. Eph 4:1–3, 8, 11–16.
20. Deut 25:14.

plants, or inanimate objects, capable in varying degrees of subduing the earth through dominion over ourselves and creation.

No one is abandoned by God, a victim of his neglect or indifference. As Paul points out to refresh the mindset of believers, the God of the Bible is generous, present, and involved with each person. We are all called by God to be human, to exercise the gifts of being kind, helpful, creative, honest, and willing. But we are not free from the responsibility to hone our skills. We are not excused from making an effort and considering the wisdom of our decisions. Our specific gifts are not gratuitous, haphazard, or random, and often are not even evident until they are explored and refined. They require no waiting around, no secret message or supernatural spark; they are part of being created in God's image and need no special intervention or creative act from him.

Chapter 12

A Lawful Yet Untidy World

We have seen that the Bible explains the tensions in our lives in a unique way. The detail differ for each of us, but there is also a commonality as we are all exposed to a world without rest, without harmony or fairness, without resolution or permanence.

On one hand, we live in an orderly, lawful, created world. There are natural laws, by which we mean that nature functions lawfully. There are also cause and effect patterns all around us that we recognize when we observe that all choices have consequences and no event occurs in a vacuum. It is very comforting to know that we live in such an orderly world. We can count on it when we know it. We can build on it and be certain that things will hold together.

On the other hand, our world is always so messy, untidy, and full of trouble! It clashes with our hopes and aspirations and disturbs our desire for well-being. Problems spark complaints as well as searches for solutions or improvements, which always bring new problems, seemingly without end. In our minds and hearts we understand what a good direction might be and how problems in our lives and daily work should be addressed and resolved. With minds and hearts, not only emotions or feelings, we analyze and comprehend enough information to listen to God's instructions and trust that he is telling the truth, to struggle for a better life, greater justice, and sound health, and diminish the results of the fall of Adam and Eve on creation and society.

The Bible gives numerous accounts of people taking their cue about all of life from what the creator and author of reality tells them. His law is the light on their path.[1] They obeyed God intellectually, rather than

---

1. Ps 119.

observing only the indications of life around them in impersonal nature or in other people's chosen views and practices.

Resourceful Opposition

The God of the Bible invites people to trust him, to pour out their pained hearts, to lament and complain, and to ask him for wisdom to cope with various situations. He has promised to be a steady help in times of trouble. From the Bible we understand why there are no easy solutions, no quick fixes, no immediate remedies. Errors and deliberate foolishness in the past bring about continuing painful results in the present because of the weight of human significance. Our own significant acts in turn can diminish these results, weaken their effect, and often channel them in a different direction. We are exposed to them but not fully defined by them, not locked into total inevitability.

What others intend for our harm may awaken our frustration and challenge our creativity so that we produce improvements or remedies. Once a problem is recognized as such, a solution can be sought, in the certain confidence that God does not ask for humble compliance, but rather courageous efforts to remedy the situation and free people from their bad experiences. Where no problem is recognized and everything accepted, no solution will be sought. Only the sick seek out a doctor.

This is first a response with our intellect, our mind, based on understanding not only what we notice in the world around us, but also what God gives us to understand. For nature can tell us facts about the present world, but not values or purposes from a longer perspective, from the beginning and into the future. Nature can show us what is, but cannot tell us what ought to be. It is a source of factual information that gives no moral guideline for which facts should be altered or accepted.

For this type of information our options are limited to personal preference, community consensus, or an indication from the Creator expressing what he had in mind. Nature is silent in these matters. Personal preference is too individualistic to be reliable. A community consensus only broadens the base, the quantity, of whatever good or bad view is advocated, but does not in itself suggest an inherent moral quality.

The missing element is only supplied by the Bible through God's informative communication in the words of the prophets, the Law of Moses and the person of His son. We should not be surprised by this dependence on intelligent instruction, since after all people are not animals or things, not nature's offspring, but God's personal creation. Only the God of the Bible has the right, and concurrent character, to instruct us and be believed. Nature says nothing about morals and purposes, and is often painful and confusing. Far from being benevolent, nature has been described by Wood Allen in one of his films as the "giant restaurant," where the big and powerful devour the small and weak.

What our minds and hearts understand from God in careful observation of nature we then express with our hands. We obey God in order to have the right kind of dominion over nature. God's word in-forms us so that we can give form to, or format, the world we live in, to dominate it and make life more possible. We decide what to plant, what tools to make, where to look for water, and what to do with it. Recognizing problems such as sickness, bad government, untrustworthy people, and vermin in our food, we are encouraged to respond practically based on God's commands. We then manage better because we are more truthful and honest about what now exists and also what should exist to benefit ourselves, others, and God.

God's work in the original creation, his words to Adam and Eve in person and to us through the Bible, and his subsequent actions and answers to prayer, all bear witness to one coherent, accessible, sensible, and sometimes surprising truth. Let me repeat that it is not religious truth, or truth about personal feelings, convictions, and hopes, but truth about the real world, real people, and real history. There is a continuity of truth between God and his creation, between his word and his actions, between what he thinks and what exists.

Requirement of Truth and Honesty

Being truthful is sadly not the primary concern in many religions and ideologies, which distract from truth and place little value on the individual mind of each person. Instead they project rich images of eternal ideals and hidden authorities outside the real world, with little connection to our present situation. Their appeal is irrational and unverifiable, and their power is rooted in the fear of people powerless to resist, yet desirous of reducing people's loneliness and pain by giving them a belief. Religions attempt to create bonds between like-minded people with common practices, using rituals with little regard for truth or reality,

A Lawful Yet Untidy World

and without respect for individuals and their minds. They create scenes, sounds, and smells but make little sense when it comes to understanding life in the real world.

Ideologies create a picture in the mind, an idea of perfection, but with very little connection to people's actual lives. They promise transformed people and circumstances in a distant future or a far away place, a "utopia," which, translating a deliberately double meaning of the Greek word, can be either *eutopia*, a "good place," or *outopia*, a "non-existing place."

Yet, in my years of observation and study I find that only the Bible truthfully honors the link between real people, real history, a real world and our demand for honest answers to the honest questions that constantly arise from our existence.

Honesty is necessary when we accept the rules agreed on for cooperation. In a game, for instance, we must follow the rules to play. Honesty establishes and maintains a firm link between words and their meaning, between promises and their execution, between labels and content, and between claims and reality. We find it in the rationality of the scientific world, in God's word, and in human communication when words carry a defined meaning. Without honesty it is impossible to relate to other people, to things in the outside world, or even one's own understanding. Dishonesty results in total isolation.

Truth and discernment are a central human need and also the central proposition about reality in the Bible.

The Bible proposes a defined, specific reality, inviting and requiring discernment, and giving the comfort of a carefully constructed certainty rather than constant instability. It tells us that it is impossible for God to lie.[2] God is therefore the "true and living God"[3] who cannot shift and change his character, who can be questioned and must give a sensible response, as he does to Job, Moses, Jeremiah, and Jesus.[4]

Truth is basic to the Bible, which starts with true distinctions, definitions, and an original antithesis: God exists rather than there being either truly nothing in existence or only an eternal presence of impersonal energy. He is the creator, not the creation. God is good in the sense that that is the definition of who he is, which he expresses in the originally orderly creation. This is not a religious claim, for its authority

---

2. Heb 6.
3. 1 Thess 1:9.
4. Job 38:1—40:2; Exod 33:14—17; John 12:27.

resides in the evidence that God does not contradict himself, nor the real world and its function.

There is simply no way to understand anything in relation to God or the world of things and people around us unless truth and honesty can be assumed between facts and ideas, and between words and meaning. This is the reason for the Ninth Commandment, which tells people not to bear false witness against one another.[5] Jeremiah laments that his people "make ready their tongue like a bow to shoot lies" and "with his mouth each speaks cordially with his neighbor, but in his heart he sets a trap for him."[6] Jesus reminds us that a "yes" should mean "yes"[7] and that we should admit we are already evil when we think evil towards others, not only when we produce evil in reality.[8] As accuracy in measures and weights is a matter of honesty, so appearance must reflect truth.

A vivid picture of our need for honesty is found in the New Testament, where we are told not be drunk with wine, but filled with the Spirit.[9] The reason for the distinction lies in the distorting effects of drunkenness, the way it slows down responses to danger and loosens the tongue from the control of careful reasoning. Loss of control leads to both physical and moral danger. By contrast, God's Spirit is described as the Spirit of Truth who will make things more clear. He helps us intellectually and morally to be truthful to what exists and to what is right and life-affirming. God's Spirit helps us discern, be wiser, more imaginative, and more responsible, all of which we need in order to stay alive in a dangerous world. God's Spirit will remind us of things we tend to forget and lead us to new truth. Through the Spirit God directs, corrects, and strengthens, confirming for us what the Spirit says in the Bible through prophets and apostles.[10]

Honesty is essential in relations between people, with each of us needing an accurate sense of our own importance, worth, and significance in both good and bad choices. History is made by us every day, and within the boundaries of past choices there is freedom to change course. We are not fully locked into the past because each day brings

---

5. Ex 20:16; Lev 19:12; Deut 5:20.
6. Jer 9:3, 8.
7. Matt 5:37.
8. Matt 5:21ff.
9. Eph 5:18.
10. 1 Pet 1:19–21.

real forgiveness as well as opportunities for new choices. We are defined as who we are before the presence of God, not by the judgment of other people. Our worth lies in being made in God's image from the start, at our beginning, not in what we may or may not become later in life through work or by the judgment of others in our society.

Notice the magnificent words of assurance at the end of the first section of Paul's letter to the church in Rome, after he has reminded them that each person of the Holy Trinity is engaged in their life. Nothing, we are told, can separate believers from the love of Christ: "If God is for us, who can be against us; he who did not spare his own son, but gave him up for us all, how will he not also . . . graciously give us all things?"[11] These are not words to support arrogance and carelessness as if nothing mattered. Instead, the significance of individual choice demands honesty because it affects the lives of everyone.

In our significance we are also prone to do wrong, to seek undue advantage, and to deceive. We are both noble and cruel. We must honestly acknowledge both moral courage and cowardice and address them with the appropriate response, neither adding nor subtracting from the fundamental value we have as people. We can do tremendous good, but are also likely to cheat, to be dishonest in the use of time and resources, take advantage of the ignorance or need of others, laugh at their plight, and decide without sufficient evidence that whatever happens to them is deserved. We should not be like Job's friends and assume that another person's suffering is God's judgment for sin. Mistrust, fear, and stifling insecurity will be the consequence when we deny the integrity of other person's complex life experience and initially and without cause consider it dishonest.

Some areas of dishonesty are obvious, such as stealing material things, someone's trust and faith, their time, investment, or money. Sometimes we simply benefit from another's ignorance. All forms of dishonesty must be recognized and combated.

We spoke earlier of the honesty of God's creation. By that we meant that things are what they were made to be; everything was made according to its kind. Nothing is accidental or unrelated, full of contradictions or unreliable. Everything has a definition from the creator and behaves accordingly. This is the basis for scientific research and progress to improve life, and it enables us to go to sleep without fear of waking up to a different world in the morning.

---

11. Rom 8:31–39.

The honesty of the natural world must also be reflected in our life and work. We must respect the structure or abilities of things and deal with them honestly. Too many buildings collapse where this is ignored, when knowledge and trust are corrupted deliberately for short term advantage. If the ratio of sand to cement required for a full chemical reaction is not respected, or the wrong wood is used for a specific structural need, when food is served, which is past its prime or has gone off, or wells are not strengthened against the eroding forces of water, or foundations are not made flexible to withstand frequent earthquakes, buildings will collapse. Many people make excuses by declaring a natural disaster when in fact there is a human disaster: deforestation, mud slides, unsafe shelters, and polluted water are often the result of human negligence or fraud, a form of dishonesty to some or all elements in a situation.

Honesty is a way of being truthful about reality, which is not random, willful, or spiteful. There should be a pleasure in the true way things work, whether in nature, in objects made and used by people, or even in language. Where truth does not matter, words will become lies and propaganda, covering up for actual indifference or deliberate misinformation, and shoddy or dishonest physical work will not stand the test of time.

Honesty, as a word and concept, is related to honor. Both words have the same root and therefore related meanings. Honesty describes the character of a relationship. It is open, reasonable, respectful, and submissive, as when we honor or respect the integrity of a person, a thing, or a situation. They all have a truthful, lawful, and defined character in the world God created. Even if this is not acknowledged, the real world is still the same and its built in definitions are still present. For that reason, rational scientific inquiry always seeks to describe the true shape of the real world.

But where other gods are believed or any transcendent orientation is denied, unthinking faith easily undermines any assurance that original definitions are true or that reality is fixed in its basic forms. Spirits, gods, or powers and will of deception play havoc with reality and rob people of basic confidence in its coherence and rationality.

Honesty is essential if we want to function well and with a clean conscience, and be good in the reality of nature, society and life under God. A deceitful or devious person is untrustworthy, a sore in the community and "an abomination to God,"[12] because falsity in word or deed

---

12. Prov 3:32.

causes disgust. Even body gestures, like a face turned away, may suggest a shifty character and dishonest ways.[13]

Truthfulness and honesty should always characterize our relationship to nature. We should always keep in mind and before our eyes, that creation is not a series of isolated things but results from someone's thoughtful and deliberate effort. Soil and water, air and plants are more than categories of *things*. Honesty requires us to know their nature and characteristics, their way of being, in order to treat them as valuable resources for life. They all have a material, some even a nutritional benefit to nourish our bodies, and they all have aesthetic qualities to engage and nurse our emotions, our moods and sense of wonder. They have an immediate usefulness but are also affected in the long term by whether we respect or misuse them.

Animals need to be studied in their manner of existence and trained to serve us well. They are not defined as lesser humans, but beings worthy of genuine respect in their own right. They fear and experience pain. They are neither divine, as in some religions, nor mere skeletons nor machines to produce meat for us. They cannot reason, but neither are they insensate like stones, water, or earth. When they are domesticated they need attention, cleanliness, the correct combination of fodder and water, and space to move about.

Domesticated means they have been bred to human proximity, and shelter is given to them so we do not leave them idle in the weather, as we may with farm equipment. Machines only need energy to be useful but animals require a constant supply of food and drink to function.

Respect for things and animals also demands that we not mistreat them. Cattle should be cleaned and given pasture, not left to stand in mud, while pigs need mud to clean themselves and to scrounge for food. Chickens need to peck though the soil for food and small grinding stones for their gizzards, so they should not be caged. Most animals need salt in one form or another. Hoofs have to be cleaned, splinters removed, and ticks lifted out and killed. Dogs need to walk or run and live in a pack, while cats are more likely to be solitary, sleeping long periods of time in warmth. Everything is of a specific kind and deserves to be treated appropriately from respect for the diversity God made. Furthermore, only human beings can be caretakers of animals in distress, including those threatened by extinction.

---

13. Prov 6:12–19; 16:27–30.

By disciplining ourselves to respect the nature of whatever is at hand we submit to the created order and remind ourselves daily that we are not lord of the manor, but servants and stewards of God and our neighbors. Each part of creation deserves to be honored for the integrity of its being and purpose. Animals must not be treated as if they were people, and people must not be treated like animals. This attitude acknowledges that we live in a world already defined, where everything is according to its kind as imagined and then created by the God of the Bible.

Protection Under the Rule of Law

The importance of honesty in our dealings with other people and the world around us is illustrated vividly when we consider the wider benefits to society under law rather than under arbitrary power.

The rule of law is an original biblical idea, rooted in the nature and character of God and his creation, and precedes all societal articulation. The only alternative is the rule of power, where the one exercising power makes law and imposes it on those under him. As natural law governs and binds all of reality, so also everyone should be subject to the same human law, thus limiting the rule of arbitrary power.

The rule of law, or the principle of *Lex Rex* (law is king), states in general terms that a set of recognized distinctions is foundational to all of life. Definitions exist at all times across all reality, grounded in the existence and character of a personal God, a Holy Trinity without confusion of persons. Distinctions are eternal, not arbitrarily chosen to control people.

Therefore law is not an afterthought, a way chosen to rule others. According to the Bible, the rule of law states that everyone, God, king, and citizen is bound to the same standard. There are no exceptions and everyone is responsible to know what is right, good, and just from perpetually existing categories that precede codified laws. The rules impose law, and the individual citizen can complain when anyone, including the ruler, acts as if he or she were above it.

There are multiple benefits of this view of law in society. It prevents havoc, uncertainty, and corruption. When powerful people, or even God, are not controlled, supervised, and limited by law, the individual lives in fear, discouraged and pressed to be dishonest as well. When the powerful can get away with exploitation, everyone else will try to exploit as well. But law holds people together around an agreed definition of life and work, of time and rewards. When it is absent, no trust can be built, no contracts honored, and no truth treasured.

The Bible tells all ruling authorities that they must read the law and also be subject to it.[14] Through the prophets God continuously reminds us that the law is a light to our path.[15] In contrast, other religions and ideologies play with power and fear, with status and formulas. When a god or the gods are not bound by law but free to behave at will, their followers will also behave in a corrupt manner to get even, seek advantage, and express their frustration in a world where only deceit leads to success.

There is a further consideration to understanding the profound benefits of law, reason, and definitions. This lawful universe, this reasonable creation with lasting definitions in all things, is echoed in the way our minds think and our eyes observe. If we do not use words that have agreed upon definitions, we can not speak with other people and be understood. When speech makes no sense and things do not follow, we become upset and are justified to complain. Our Conscience alerts us when we contradict ourselves, when what we do does not agree with what we say, or when we change our mind or values without explanation.

We realize that we should not behave this way, because it contradicts the logical workings of the world around us and the internal structures, the grammar of our brain and memory. We are no longer at peace, but bewildered, worried, and fearful that we may be discovered, that the truth may come out. We have become guilty through our inconsistencies, broken promises, and false claims of authority.

Honesty toward the shape of the real world requires that we honor our spouse, children, and neighbors. Our commitments and promises to them are deliberate efforts, like other binding covenants, to limit our opportunities to break the sacred bond of marriage, do evil, and betray trust in human and work relationships. Dishonesty is a form of deceit, pretense, or make believe, an always present temptation that we must avoid because of the damage, uncertainty, and suspicion it creates in personal relations and public life. Dishonesty can destroy the unique intimacy of marriage, which is based on the reality that each person is conceived in the physical intimacy of one father and one mother. So too dishonesty can destroy trust in a person's word in business relationships. A craftsman's reputation is ruined if it is found out that he uses dishonest

---

14. E.g. Neh 8: 2; Chron 34:15–21.
15. Ps 119.

measures and weights or falsifies documents to show only the external appearance of his work rather than its inner quality.

All these reflections bear on how important it is that our word is a clear yes or no, without confusion or deception. The profound and wide reaching meaning and value of honesty is concentrated in these two short words we use so often. Without a precise, honest meaning, their deceptive use brings down the whole structure of confidence needed for marriage, family, lasting trust, and life in society.

Do all these considerations make life nothing but a burden? Is there a shortcut to a better life without constant reminders of what is true, good, and just?

We shall address these questions with the answers we find thanks to our uniquely capable mind: by thinking further about them in light of reality and the Bible, resisting subservience to our natural and unreflective human impulses of the moment.

Chapter 13

Wisdom from Proverbs

EVERYTHING WE HAVE so far considered confirms that life is hard and multiple hindrances obstruct the path to satisfaction, peace, beauty, and justice. But we have also seen how the Bible gives human beings a high calling to work with minds and hands to create a larger context for life, to discern between opposites like good and evil, life and death, true and false, valuable and wasteful, rather than to "go with the flow" or wait until things change by themselves, if ever.

The Bible indicates this by asserting that people are made in the image of the Creator. In our physical bodies and with only limited knowledge we are unlike God, and since the fall of Adam and Eve we are also guilty and our whole being is damaged. But we are still like God in our ability to think, imagine, evaluate differences, and understand. We have a mind that is more than a tool, for it is creative, has memory, and can doubt.

I have suggested that making choices is part of our nature and integral to the mandate from God to have dominion. It explains why our calling is to discern, to review and possibly change the current situation. Unlike a leaf that simply falls off a tree in the autumn and is then carried away by currents in the river, we go places in our mind by imagining possible alternatives, and we explore our physical setting and look around for more advantageous situations.

"We have not, because we ask not"[1] describes so many cases where people are the victims of their natural, political, and social circumstances. They bow to what is around them and give up the search for what ought to be. They assume that whatever exists is right and whatever happens in fact inevitable. By giving up on an intellectual and spiritual framework

1. Jas 4:2.

that calls for review of the current situation, they forego moral judgment and remain ignorant of the Bible's uniquely different perspective. For them, the heavens are closed and silent, but for Jews and Christians God has spoken, explained things, and come to be among us and value us in all areas of existence.

The book of Proverbs is a very practical and rich source of insights into what everyone encounters in daily life in society and every family. Proverbs offers wisdom and knowledge to facilitate personal relationships, showing what is prudent and helpful to achieve a congenial way of life in community. It assumes that we can learn from the errors and the wisdom of the past in order to think rationally into the future so that we will know what to do and what to avoid. With wisdom in poetic form and vivid imagery, Proverbs teaches that subservience to natural and human powers need not be our experience. Human beings should be proactive, always searching, listening, and weighing possibilities and alternatives. For our bodies are tied to earth, but our mind, heart, and soul show that we are human beings made in the image of God.

"If you accept my words and store up my commands within you, turning your ear to wisdom and applying your heart to understanding and if you call out for insight and cry aloud for understanding and if you look for it as for silver and search for it as for hidden treasure, then you will understand the fear of the Lord and find the knowledge of God."[2]

The Bible orients us our minds, heart and knowledge as people to the mind and purposes of the personal God, giving the only answer to the question of human origins and character that honors people. It rejects any merger with nature, history, or the firmament of the sun, moon, and stars. This view, which was pervasive in pagan religions in the past, is today embraced by a wide majority of people who do not know God nor themselves as his image bearers, who believe instead that they have evolved to become very complex animals, but animals all the same. This leads them to a low view of humanity and leaves the crucial questions of justice, purpose, and life and death to whatever wishful thinking they choose to embrace.

At the core of our personality and significance we are choice-makers. We choose all manner of things, situations, words and works, relationships and behavior. Every choice requires effort, deliberation, and change if there are to be results. Choices set people free from the

---

2. Prov 2:1–5.

dictates of circumstance and reveal the uniqueness of each individual. When people fail to think and act this way, poverty, discouragement, and suffering are the result.

With choices also come difficulties, especially in a fallen world. There are the frustrations we experience in our arrangements for living, the culture we were born into, and the limitations due to external factors such as geography. There is lack of learning and the wish that we were already further ahead, more capable, with greater insight and better tools. We may also lack resources and face an uncertain legal status without the safety of a stable political or social situation.

The Bible knows all kinds of hindrances to a better life, describing the frustrations of both individuals and governments. And yet it also shows the way ahead through responsible steps and moral insistence and then perseverance.

Scripture prescribes steps to diminish the pain and agony of life in this fallen world. It also describes what people have done to improve their situation: Isaac dug a well for irrigation;[3] Abigail met David to reason with him in the hope of calming down his anger;[4] and Nehemiah set out to rebuild the walls of Jerusalem against much internal and external opposition.[5] The New Testament assumes human effort in the working background of people in many of the parables: fishermen, carpenters, farmers, shepherds, traders, teachers, and lawyers, and public officials.

The wise insight in the book of Proverbs reminds us, in poetic form, of real hardships and the efforts necessary to diminish them and their causes. Things do not simply improve with time. To bring about substantial change we need personal effort, a sound mind, clear purpose, and a determined will to improve the quality of life.

The key to improvement is always hard thoughtful intellectual and manual work.[6] Such work gives us tools to escape the trap of ignorance, social settings, and fear, of simply waiting to see what happens. Work is hard because it does not happen by itself; it must be chosen in response to God's mandate to have dominion and resist what has become so normal in this broken world.

---

3. Gen 26.
4. 1 Sam 25.
5. Neh 2:11—13:32.
6. Prov 6:4–5, 9–11.

Only personal effort makes a better situation possible, for nothing will improve by itself. Fruit trees must be trimmed and pruned, and directed by human effort, to produce well Fields need to be cleared of weeds, and seeds need a dry and dark place for storage before the next planting season. Food storage must be protected from mice, and disease carrying flies must be kept away from human beings and what they eat. Refrigeration prevents decay, and filtering systems purify drinking water. Roads need to be safe for farmers to travel to market.

The desire to communicate over long distances has led to improved technology and ever new ways to send signals, words, and pictures. Such efforts apply human insight and factual/moral discernment to transform impersonal nature. Lack of effort and a slack hand make one poor because they accomplish little; diligence in both physical and mental work provides a surplus over basic needs.[7]

The book of Proverbs is full of colorful examples that give us encouragement and a grounding in realism. The employer and hired hand both need to pull their weight as a team, lest the employer becomes annoyed with an idle or lazy employee, who in turn resents his absent boss.[8] Fair wages must be matched by fair performance as part of the contract between two parties committed to shared and complimentary efforts between them. The job must be well done as required, uninterrupted by daydreaming, fantasies, and other distractions.[9] Work should produce results and be as satisfying as possible, showing forth human significance and responsibility. Faithful people who act from accountability to self and others can be trusted and gradually given more authority. They will work even when not supervised.

By contrast, a lazy person who is resentful, unmotivated, and always in need of supervision will remain in constant servitude.[10] Such a person is like the hunter who stops his work before he has roasted his game. He is enthused briefly with the power of the hunt but does not enjoy what he has accomplished and loses the benefit of his work.[11] Lazy people may desire a better life but rarely attain it. They want to get somewhere without walking, acquire knowledge without study, and develop relationships

---

7. Prov 10:4.
8. Prov 10:26.
9. Prov 12:11.
10. Prov 12:24.
11. Prov 12:27.

without becoming interesting and trustworthy. They want the prize without the effort. They never realize that the hindrance to success is their own attitude or failure to understand how reality functions in its cause and effect structure. They want only the prize without any effort.

However, "the righteous hate what is false."[12] They are diligent and understand that things are accomplished only through determined, careful, and lasting work. There is profit in all work, but when it is reduced to mere talk about possibilities it often results in poverty.[13] Only the interaction between conversation about ideas and the follow-up efforts in practice brings about real results. Talk is always abstract and requires the hard soil of life to be proven right or wrong. Telling stories may stimulate the mind and prod the hand to action, but can also be a distraction from the requirements of life in the real world. Stories can create fear, envy, and resentment as often as they can stimulate enterprise.

A vivid picture of the person caught in a patch of thorns illustrates the difference between sloth and diligence. Instead of clearing the patch and keeping an eye on its fast growth, the lazy person spends his time thinking of other things and so becomes entangled in the thorns. But the diligent person who is engaged with the reality of present needs has pruned back the thorns and moves freely.[14] The desire to accomplish a task is like a hunger that drives him on, giving the motivation to step out of the circle of repetition into a straight line of work,[15] and pursue his intent through creative intervention. Envisaging the goal clarifies how to pursue its immediate demands to achieve the intended result. Everything else, like complaining and moping about, plotting evil, or gossiping about others, will accomplish nothing and prevent all benefits.

People often blame God for the troubles they bring on themselves.[16] Laziness is actually a form of destruction,[17] of missed opportunities. It makes a person stand still rather than move and grow. It destroys by omission, failing to accomplish something good and useful. A clear example of this is given in the proverb that idleness brings hunger[18]: the picture

12. Prov 13:4ff.
13. Prov 14:23.
14. Prov 15:19.
15. Prov 16:26–28.
16. Prov 19:3.
17. Prov 18:9.
18. Prov 19:15, 24.

is of a person who, having his head in the bowl of food, is too lazy to eat from it. God has not given us rest so that we can be lazy, but to prepare us for our next fruitful activity.[19] The purpose of sleep is not to avoid work, but to renew our strength and power of concentration.

A lazy person may have plenty of desires yet make no effort to achieve them in practice.[20] This is illustrated in a humorous way in the proverb of the man who begs off or withdraws from work, crying out about a danger, but then does nothing to disarm the threat. He is like a door swaying in the wind or a person who turns over in his bed but doesn't get up.[21] Instead, we should deal with issues in a realistic manner, not pursuing things that make no sense or are vain. Following pipe dreams only impoverishes.[22]

The book of Proverbs addresses these issues of work and idleness, their logical and practical consequences, in the form of poetry. Rather than providing simple prescriptions, Proverbs creates memorable reminders in form and content which become images of what contributes to or hinders the functioning of society, business, and other human relationships.

The Importance of Morals and Ethics

We should remember that honesty is founded in the coherent, rational structure of reality. The world is constructed by a thinking God so that the things in it remain honest to their character, shape, or designation. Honesty is a moral obligation based on acknowledgment of factual restraints. There is no other world to live in and there is no other way for social relations to function well.[23]

Honesty allows us safe sleep undisturbed by nightmares and free from terror caused by fear and guilt. Honesty also obliges us to quickly return things held in trust, to refuse to scheme against someone who relies on us, and to avoid an uncaused quarrel.[24] The prosperity of sinners

---

19. Prov 20:12–13.
20. Prov 13:4; 21:25–26a.
21. Prov 26:14–15.
22. Prov 28:19.
23. Prov 3:21–35.
24. Prov 3:29ff.

must not be envied.[25] God respects a straightforward person, while a devious one is an abomination to any neighbor.[26]

Weakness of character makes people untrustworthy. Their word cannot be relied on. Physical signs like nervously avoiding eye contact, shuffling of feet, or wild gesticulations can reveal duplicity of heart, a lying tongue that incites quarrels, and "feet quick to run to evil."[27] The problem is that deception often parades as truth and folly mimics wisdom, but always with the opposite effect.[28] Wrongly gained advantages will be of no use beyond the temporary appearance of wealth and power. Only righteousness will outlast general disaster, as it can never be taken away.[29]

Honesty must also be the goal in other relations, even when we are exposed to multiple threats like ridicule or bribery in business or by regulatory agencies. We may want to succumb to temptation and act dishonestly. Bribery, both active and passive, destroys the rule of law between people by making exceptions for individuals and currying favor; it is one of the great scourges in societies where law is disregarded. Bribes pervert justice for money, changing well defined practices based on common rights and obligations into merely personal exchanges.[30] They change agreed and defined practices, rights and obligations into personal, undefined and altered ones. In distinction to gifts that require no return, bribes trade special influence for personal favors outside of law. They distort reality by introducing the unpredictable participation of influence peddlers into the market, thereby destroying the very notion of equal law for all people.[31] Bribes create insecurity, favoritism, and partiality.[32] To act above or free from the law is arrogant and lacks integrity. "The deviousness of the treacherous leads them to ruin. Wealth is of no avail on the day of wrath,"[33] which often takes the form of social unrest and bloody revolutions.

We are also reminded in Proverbs that the stability of commerce requires reliable weights and measures, perhaps the most common means to

---

25. Prov 3:31.
26. Prov 3:32.
27. Prov 6:12–19.
28. Prov 9:16b–17.
29. Prov 10:2a; see also Ezek 7:19.
30. Prov 17:23.
31. Prov 15:27b.
32. Prov 18:5.
33. Prov 11:3.

be truthful or to deceive. For our culture of packaged goods the equivalent would be the insistence on accurate labeling Using alternate weights, larger or smaller, or deceptive advertising, is a lie and a form of bribery, to gain an advantage for one side and diminish the benefit for the other. Customers should receive the full value they bargain for,[34] both in money paid as well as in quality received. Money is easily devalued through inflation, and poor quality easily hidden behind an attractive appearance, deceptive packaging, or a flattering but dishonest description. Both distortions are forms of theft that count on the ignorance of the trading partner and pretend a commensurate benefit for everyone involved.

Proverbs condemns those who distort reality through pretence, pointing out that a man of crooked mind comes to no good, and he who speaks duplicity falls into trouble. Such schemers will be found out and their reputation tarnished. They may be feared but not honored or loved.[35] In its poetic imagery, Proverbs makes clear that the pleasure and sweetness of theft do not last: the titillating pleasures of fraudulent gain may be tasty at first, but will later fill the mouth with gravel.[36]

Further distortion comes from a lying tongue when false words replace accurate speech. Whatever is gained through lies is like vapor, ephemeral, and in the end a deadly trap.[37] For this reason a good reputation for honesty in speech, practical dealings, commerce, and all other relationships is preferable to a position of wealth, power, and status gained through deceit.[38]

An honest person's reputation built on solid ground stands firm regardless of external circumstances and brings with it a good conscience and lasting value. But the deceiver lives in constant fear of being found out; his reputation is built on pretense and lasts only as long as his lies and corruption are not unmasked.[39] His house built of playing cards is easily flattened by a slight disturbance and provides no lasting shelter. The biblical picture of such a life of dishonesty and pretence is of a house built on sand rather than rock: when the rains come it will be washed away, while the house built on the Rock will remain standing.[40]

34. Prov 11:1; 16:11; 20:10; Amos 8:5; Deut 25:13.
35. Prov 17:20.
36. Prov 20:17; 9:17b.
37. Prov 21:6.
38. Prov 22:1.
39. Prov 28:6.
40. Matt 7:24–27.

Chapter 14

A House on Solid Rock

THE HOUSE BUILT ON solid rock, able to withstand the storms of life and our floods of tears and doubt is a picture of Christian confidence. It is not an image of mere faith or a personal belief, but rather the sure knowledge of rock solid reality and its Creator.

This view may at first be a surprise, yet the biblical understanding of faith is being sure of what we hope for and having certainty in things not yet fully seen. It is not make believe, but the recognition that God "exists and that he rewards those who earnestly seek him."[1] Faith in God, according to the Bible, is the acknowledgment that truth and reality are accessible to the critical mind, and that God does not lie about anything: himself first, then the reality of the universe around us, and finally human beings.

Our confidence is therefore in the reality of truth: facts on the ground, laws in all natural things, people as people, and the visible work of God, the Creator and our maker. The Bible gives an accurate description of the nature of reality: we live in a world of real things, people, and events, in a condition of true moral guilt for objective wrong we knowingly have done. God has responded to make himself known and to address that moral failure; from the time he ran after Adam and Eve and called them to repentance and a new direction in life, there is abundant evidence of God's care and compassion for the human situation.

That is what we believe and why the "fear of the Lord"—our respect for God and enjoyment of him—brings security. Self-reliance, or making up our own story about what reality is like, where people come from, and

---

1. Heb 11:1–6.

what the gods tell us, brings disaster.[2] In his letter to the Colossians, Paul prays that our knowledge of God will increase,[3] and that we understand the wholeness of life more fully. All the words of the prophets and apostles have this same purpose; they all should be read as "letters from God," because they explain our situation and the possibilities in front of us.

The Bible: Clarity About Reality

The Bible is much more than a collection of separate verses or a set of moral prescriptions; it is, rather, a whole statement about reality. Not a mere story among others, the Bible provides the glasses to resolve our difficulty in clearly seeing reality, so that life and purpose come into proper focus and can be truly discerned with intellectual honesty.

The letter to the Hebrews gives an account of people in the Bible who acted on the basis of what they understood and believed and how they benefited from it. Abel's sacrifice was accepted by God, because it followed God's instruction, Noah survived the flood, and Abraham and Sarah settled in what would become the homeland of the Jewish nation and people, even though in their old age they had no children.

This understanding of the person and promises of God has given confidence, meaning, and moral orientation to Jews and Christians throughout history. With the knowledge of God in their heads and the love of God in their hearts they have repeatedly stood against inherited, flawed, fatalistic views of reality. They did not passively submit to circumstances, but were willing to grapple with issues of ignorance, freedom, justice and health. They were carried forward by the desire for a better life of work and creativity, so that they could try to overcome obstacles in nature and among rulers, priests, and kings. Their security lay in the knowledge of God, while those around them ignored or at times even hated God and preferred to live in the repetition of nature's cycles, tribal traditions, or social customs. Yet anyone who refuses God's advice will eat the fruit of their ways, their choices, their fears. Repetition gives an illusion of insight because everyone participates. But without review and the possibility for improvement, the illusion becomes more important than actually coping with a complex and dangerous reality.

Proverbs asks,

2. Prov 1:29–33.
3. Col 1:9–14.

> How long will you simple ones love simplicity . . . you dullards hate knowledge? . . . You spurned all my advice and would not hear my rebuke. I will laugh at your calamity, and mock when terror comes upon you. . . . They refused my advice and disdained all my rebukes. . . . The tranquility of the simple will kill them and the complacency of the dullards will destroy them. But he who listens to me will dwell in safety, untroubled by the terror of the misfortune.[4]

This text does not promise a life free from danger, but reminds us that our confidence lies in God not in gain, which may be little or prove transitory, "fly away."

Because we have this wider biblical understanding of the difficulties and unfairness of life we are called to extra truthfulness, kindness, and self-control. We should act only after reflection. Habit, natural inclination, and opportunity are not in themselves good guides to action. We must consider and confront the possibility of fearful future consequences to ourselves and our children first, and eventually also from God. Self-control and personal discipline single us out as individuals, express and mold our character, and establish our name and reputation. Self-control should be exercised in moral and economic choices, shaping the way we live and work as we apply a deeper understanding of our calling from God to daily action.

Illustrations from the natural world reveal how essential it is to be disciplined rather than being driven by circumstances. Even the ant without a mind provides for the future through hard work now.[5] Discipline enables us to make use of time and the seasons of the year, otherwise poverty ensues, for fields will be overgrown with weeds and water will run away unused. Some people enjoy lounging in bed rather than getting up,[6] or prefer community celebrations sharing stories with amusing neighbors instead of a hard day's work; in some cultures long religious festivals steal time away from necessary work, which remains undone. In each case "poverty will come calling upon you," often the consequence of an undisciplined life not in accord with the shape of reality, God's instructions, and rational insight into how work, time, effort, knowledge, and learned skills cohere in a meaningful human existence.[7]

4. Prov 1:25, 26, 29–33.
5. Prov 6:6–8.
6. Prov 6:9–11; 24:30–34.
7. Prov 15:31.

Part of the problem is lack of humility, our unwillingness to admit that we need to learn from God and others how reality proceeds in its created and scientific rationality in the coherence of reality. Humility is not good when it is based on denial of one's importance to God, to life, and to others. It is, however, essential for those who are willing to understand more and have their errors corrected. Admitting the need to learn helps avoid poverty and disgrace.[8] Like work that dirties your hands yet rewards you with benefits, or like an ox that soils its stable but also brings in the harvest,[9] humility may seem initially degrading as you admit how little you know, but it is the first step in finding the necessary courage and enterprise to gain knowledge. Later humility cedes the place to knowledge, courage, and enterprise. In contrast, the proud boast of their clever ways but eventually fail for lack of openness to new challenges.[10] So too false humility hinders the benefit of useful knowledge.

"The greatest hindrance to knowledge is the belief that one already knows."[11] The reward for humbly admitting ignorance and seeking understanding through an open mind, hard work, and the admission of one's own need is honor, and life, and at times, but without guarantee, also riches.[12] These things will follow as a natural and logical consequence. By contrast, a person with overconfidence is often intellectually and morally lazy, smug, and conceited.[13]

Generosity toward others is also a kind of humility. It reflects the realization that we live in the rich, diverse, and fruitful world originally created by a generous God who now instructs us to help repair its damage and to anticipate his restored Kingdom on earth. The habit of generosity expresses that we find our worth and position not in the things we own but in the character we exhibit through kindness, compassion, and involvement in the needy lives of neighbors.[14]

Generosity means helping people in the community rather than caring only for oneself. That is precisely the difference between generosity and

---

8. Prov 13:18.
9. Prov 14:4.
10. Prov 16:18-19.
11. Daniel Boorstin's *The Discoverers* (Vintage, 1985), xv. He adds, "The great obstacle to discover the shape of the earth was not ignorance, but the illusion of knowledge" (86).
12. Prov 22:4.
13. Prov 26:16.
14. Luke 10:25-37; Matt 22:34-40.

greed.[15] There is also opposition between speaking favorably and wicked speech; between being contemptuous and prudent; keeping matters in confidence instead of giving away secrets; being graceful, kind and "sowing righteousness" rather than being ruthless, cruel, and wicked. These contrasts are set out as examples that warn against a naïveté often found among people desiring to be generous: "harm awaits him who stands surety for another, a stranger, and he who spurns pledging shall be secure."[16]

Generosity as a life habit reflects our understanding of God's generosity to us in life. It is one way to diminish the evil that results from life in this fallen world. God's generosity is both material in the natural abundance he created, and intellectual/spiritual in the instructions, directions, and explanations he gives us. Our generosity honors God when we do his work of comforting, healing, and feeding with our material wealth as well as our wealth of insight. Generosity is not only practiced when we give away our surplus, but also when we invest in enterprises to create jobs and hire workers, facilitating markets, transport, and exchanges. It is also practiced when we provide for education of the mind in schools, when we build clinics for the body, and when we pay taxes for a government under law to protect and enable civil society with law.

Such generosity will have beneficial results across the whole of our lives and to future generations.[17]

This link between generosity and benefit is perhaps unexpected but not illogical. Generosity today may lead to loss but then return as future rewards and profit because of the order of God's world. There will be no new crop unless part of last year's harvest is sown on the field for the future.[18] God honors generosity, while stinginess only increases want.[19] A generous man knows that future diligence can replace what he gives away without stint.[20]

Generosity is also a way to diminish the unfairness of life. We should engage people not on the basis of what they have, but who they are in their present situation. Rather than despising people in need, we should see them as a possible source for our greater happiness, because

15. Prov 1:11–19.
16. Prov 1:15.
17. Prov 3:9–10.
18. John 12:24: "Unless a corn of wheat fall into the ground . . . it remains single. But if it dies it produces many seeds."
19. Prov 11:24–26.
20. Prov 21:26b.

we can help diminish their hardship.[21] Such generosity honors God[22] for it is the kind of work he wants us to accomplish in dominion over creation, our own greed, and the basic unfairness of life. When a need is recognized and something concrete done in response, the members of a household are not deprived but rather enriched by the development of their character. Through generosity we improve human existence rather than merely observing and accepting the circumstances we encounter. Investing material resources or benefits in people will bring a rich personal, moral, and cultural return.

A greedy person can harm his family by preventing their exposure to the frequently tragic reality of life, so they never experience the changed attitudes, lives, and relationships their generous help can produce.[23] The Bible sees generosity to the poor as a loan to God, who promises to repay the lender.[24] He normally uses the agency of human beings to accomplish his work: the baker is the person through whom God gives us bread, and the judge is the person through whom law protects us against arbitrary power.

A wealthy man may be stingy, leading an empty, heartless life,[25] so we should not desire to be in his shoes. Wealth may hinder interaction with people, just like too much sweet honey overwhelms our taste buds and may choke us to the point of throwing up.[26] It is difficult for the wealthy to distinguish between the sincere friendship of others and envy masquerading as affection and closeness. Wealthy people may stir up strife rather than genuine admiration and will be resented when focus on their wealth distances them from neighbors. This kind of prosperity will bring little joy to the wealthy and only fear, hostility, and disrespect from others.[27]

Instead, wealth gained by legal and moral means—not exploiting another's dependent situation through excessive interest on loans or reduced remuneration by exploiting market conditions—should be the

---

21. Prov 14:21.
22. Prov 14:31.
23. Prov 15:27a.
24. Prov 19:17.
25. Prov 23:6–7.
26. Prov 25:16.
27. Prov 28:25.

source of generosity to the poor.[28] Generosity to the genuinely needy will not impoverish; but willful hardness of heart in the face of poverty breeds material and social injustice, and brings with it a breakdown of trust, admiration, dependence, and other valuable components of human relationships.[29]

In summary, God sets out and approves the basic components of good work habits and commercial interaction. Whether in relation to God, to whom all hearts are open and all things are known,[30] or in relation to the orderly creation, honesty, integrity, and faithfulness are of primary importance.

Integrity is required of us because of the character of God and the nature of creation. Both God and his creation will evaluate and judge what we think and do. Both are consistent, undivided, non-contradictory, and reliable, while we are choice makers and can therefore err. We must choose to be without contradiction, honest and faithful in our moral character. Paul writes that we, as children of God, should be without blame,[31] above reproach, and cut no corners. We must avoid rationalizing our behavior to justify any means for the sake of a desirable end.

In practice this means that we should carefully distinguish all the ways people act dishonestly, when they cheat, do not keep their word, and break contracts. We are blameless when we meet our contractual obligations, work hard, and do not steal our employer's time through tardiness or carelessly contracted illness. Taking office supplies, postage, making personal phone calls, and taking too many breaks for personal use are also forms of theft, as is cheating on taxes, even if the government is corrupt.[32]

There will be no long term benefit when trust is violated, quality is compromised, or appearances deceive. There will be no spiritual fruitfulness if we are dishonorable in business, human relations, and family commitments.[33] The result will rarely be a divine intervention of God's judgment but there will always be logical, material, and cultural consequences when people fail to be truthful to the laws of cause and effect God created.

28. Prov 28:8.
29. Prov 28:27.
30. Ps 44:21.
31. Phil 2:15.
32. Matt 22:18–21.
33. Luke 16:10ff.

In practice, accounting will be inaccurate, profit diminished, and trust between employees damaged. Suspicion, secrets, and disrespect will grow quickly and affect future generations. When children see their parents' immoral behavior they will, from respect and admiration, assume it is justified and copy it, and develop an attitude that we all have the right to whatever we can get away with. To diminish this behavior and to reveal the facts, all light bulbs and coat hangers in my father's business bore the label: "Stolen from (the name of his company)."

Therefore, in addition to being blameless, we should also be innocent—pure to the core with God's standards directing our hearts with understanding and conviction. Noah is exemplary as a righteous man who did not behave in the manner of his neighbors, did not do what were their patterns, but stood out from the crowd for his integrity before God and the world. The same characteristic is also seen in Job, where it is very important to understand from the outset that his friends' accusations are wrong.[34] Job is declared righteous by God, demonstrating that his sufferings did not indicate responsibility for personal moral guilt.

To that end we should adopt an attitude of careful inquiry, of hesitation and skepticism before we agree to do something, always weighing arguments and comparing new ideas, observations, and possible practices with what we already know from the workings of reality. Scientific insight and knowledge always increases, but that is a question of the *quantity* of knowledge, of progress and greater efficiency, and what is possible in the real world.

Moral and practical decisions about what to do and what to leave alone must be examined from a concern not for *quantity*, but rather *quality*, character, and consequences. These are different concerns that relate to what should be done or left undone. Wrong choices here will lead to guilt, harm, and waste. We live in a world of malicious forces eager to devour our integrity and moral compass, where something can be justified simply because it can be done and where only material facts limit human actions. This is "possibility thinking," taking advantage of every possibility without restraints derived from moral considerations.

In this social and intellectual climate, the moral dimension of respect for people, human rights, and social justice has been largely reduced to personal convictions, if not wholly eliminated. Yet any complaint and call for justice, respect, and recompense needs a moral justification to

---

34. Gen 6:9 and Job 1:1.

be taken seriously. Morality prescribes behavior and calls for correction, while possibilities by themselves are neutral, factual, and without compulsion. In a world viewed without a moral dimension there is no room for complaint, accusation, praise, or blame. Among the possible alternatives, only the Bible gives a moral base and obligations for each person in the exercise of freedom among factual alternative possibilities.

In such a cultural context we must be like serpents, masters of strategy, canny, prudent, and wise about the ways of the world.[35] Simultaneously, we must be innocent as doves that do not shut their eyes to danger, but pay careful attention and wisely fly away. Both attitudes should characterize us as God's children, set apart to a life of integrity, holiness, and moral purity, distant from what is common practice. We are set apart for God's use (the moral obligation) in all ours dealings with work, people, the environment, and money, which are all in the realm of practical possibilities for improvement.

It is sensible for us to live committed to the truth of the world so that as God's people we are open to a more accurate reading of the means and purposes of existence. We can be honest about people and address their practical needs with energy, imagination, daring, and innovation because the Bible gives us a comprehensive moral framework. We do not expect perfection in morals or in practice, seek short-term goals, or need pretence. We realize the need for compassion in our families as well as our businesses, and daily contacts. As Jesus is the exact representation of the invisible God,[36] our whole lives, including our business relations and practices, should tell people that we understand life realistically, based on the present condition of the created world[37] and God's character as Jesus exhibited it in his life.

To understand life in all its complexity is not a fundamentally "religious" pursuit; instead, it is simply to be truthful, to act with integrity, and to not give occasion to be blamed for wrong by God or our fellow humans. God calls us to enjoy ourselves as he made us to be human, reasonable, and able to do good work in spite of the crooked and twisted natural and human reality surrounding people in every generation.[38] We

---

35. Matt 10:16.
36. Heb 1:3.
37. Col 1:15ff.
38. Deut 32:5.

do not need to listen to the opinions of our neighbors except when they also try to stay truthful to reality.

God's straight and narrow path[39] is to believe what he tells us about the world and respond by practicing right[40] behavior. We must reject the waywardness of an erroneous outlook on the world, focusing instead on God's way, for he authored, created, and purposed it. Other beliefs are wrong not because they are different but because they are in so many ways incompatible with the shape and nature of reality. Religions gather adherents around ideas and relate them to a common practice, but that in itself is no evidence of the truth and accuracy of those ideas and practices when they are measured in light of how reality works. Like opium or other drugs they often distort and abolish reality.

Neither the natural world nor human reality tolerates a private reading or personal faith, ideology, or wishful interpretation. The world already exists and functions in a coherent manner regardless of our personal preferences, illusions, or religions; to disregard its shape and functioning leads to pain and death. The true knowledge of reality brings about favorable results to anyone conforming to it, but like poison which kills someone despite his intense personal convictions, an inaccurate or superficial reading of reality leads to painful results for those who follow it.

Voluntary submission to the authority of God and the natural functioning of his creation may disturb our sense of moral autonomy. But we need not see it as a loss, an abandonment of personal identity, if we keep in mind that we appear late in a history that began much earlier. Other forms of submission are similar. Husbands and wives are to love and serve one another. Their life together is richer than each life alone but can only be enjoyed when each honors the other. Men leave their parents to join their wives, and when wives are instructed to be subject to their husbands, the text also says that husbands ought to give themselves to their wives.[41] The picture is one of love, mutual benefit, and service. In fact, the Bible warns us that after the fall and the damage it did to all reality, men will rule over women.[42] That is not a command, but a lament over the sinful exploitation of others. And indeed many men mistreat

---

39. Matt 7:13.

40. Matt 5:20. Righteousness here and in Gen 6:9 and Job 1:1 is related to what is right, e.g. correct weights and measures in Lev 19:35. It deals with right thinking and practices first, and then also belief.

41. Gen 2:24 and Eph 5:22ff.

42. Gen 3:16.

women in most cultures not influenced by Christianity, where they use their wives as personal property.

Similarly, employees are to submit to their employers, who define job expectations and set payment, whether in cash or in kind. The Bible even addresses slaves, admonishing them to faithful work.[43] However, in contrast to slaves in ancient Roman or modern times, they were not without rights and protections. They were like indentured servants or bondmen with the status of hired laborers, who would be freed after six years[44] in the master's household.[45] The Bible demands humane treatment based on the shared humanity of master and servant or slave, so that there are moral safeguards when one indentures himself for financial support, or as a way for a convicted thief to pay back what he owes, or for a debtor to work off defaulted loans.[46]

In all cases, servants, slaves, hired hands, or employees, whether their work is a fulfilling delight or a boring necessity must submit to their masters and accept authority in all things related to the work. Both master and employee should please one another each of them is a resource for life to the other: the employer because he gets work done for his benefit, and the employee because he earns the means for life and a measure of satisfaction.[47] More is required of both than doing as little as possible to get by, whether in pay or performance, and not angering each other.

In such a relationship the focus on common humanity requires respect for basic, undeniable rights and privileges. Paul goes so far as to suggest that if a runaway slave becomes a believer he should return to his master who must then receive him as a brother.[48]

Paul points out that submission involves accepting authority at the work place, respecting ownership, and therefore not pilfering. To respect authority of the employer does not entail giving up something, but rather acknowledging in good faith that one's responsibility is derived and giving him full value for the wages he pays and the trust he extends.

Such submission shows that we properly understand what life in a fallen yet defined world requires, and accept the validity and the benefits

---

43. Titus 2:9–10.
44. Exod 21:2–6.
45. Exod 12:44.
46. 2 Kgs 4:1; Neh 5:1–6.
47. Titus 2:9ff.
48. Phlm 15.

of instructions received from God. Even someone without an immediate boss must follow the same principle of submission to God and the unchangeable aspects of reality. There are no independent, self-made people anywhere, so we must admit that we always have someone to serve.

Because of our forgetfulness and the ease with which we make excuses for our choices, it is important to remind ourselves continually of the wisdom of God's instructions. Our surroundings offer tempting distractions and vivid images as alternatives, so we must discipline our thoughts and actions and, like good scientists, study all reality to review our understanding and correct our behavior when we discover error and false conclusions.

Such destructive alternatives are presented in all aspects of our lives and the apparent advantage they offer too easily seduces us. Sexual temptations and financial dishonesty are perhaps the most dominant, because both realms are so central to our experiences and needs. Sexual sins harm other people by destroying respect and intimacy; money sins destroy the integrity of business and the work place. Both of these areas of easy temptation are also called "the flesh" and "the world," which have nothing to do with the wonder of the human body or the reality of a created world. Instead, they describe "the craving of sinful man, the lust of his eyes and the boasting of what he has and does." The craving and the boasting are what is meant by "the world and its desires, (which) pass away."[49]

Our best defense against sin is reverence for God's Word and its instructions, insights, and advice.[50] It is not a spiritual or blind reverence but one based on appreciation for the truth, relevance, and accuracy of the Bible. In Proverbs, the attractiveness of a harlot contrasts with the wisdom of God's word.[51] The naïve young man who is attracted to the harlot lacks good sense because intimacy with God's wisdom, "the apple of your eye," is truly desirable. The intimacy of knowing God and his will diminishes the tempting intimacy of a fleeting night of pleasure. The former leads to life, the latter eventually to death. God's word should guide our hands and actions as well as our thoughts and motivations, our heart.

The lesson in Proverbs is that life requires common sense, instructed by God's word not as a religious motivation but because it gives knowledge of how reality, including human sexual reality, functions. Morality has

---

49. 1 John 2:16–17.
50. Prov 7:1–5.
51. Prov 7:3–27.

practical implications and should lead to realism. But instead of disciplining his desire, the inexperienced young man in Proverbs deliberately flirts with temptation by crossing the street in the cover of dusk and accepting the harlot's attention. He is simple, young, and senseless, and she preys on him and pounces like a beast, deceiving him with charming words.

All of us—alcoholics, accountants, people in sales, religious leaders, and others—similarly justify our destructive actions with ease. For short-term gain we disregard long-term effects. Without the discipline and insight of God's word we are attracted by seeming benefits, unaware of the eventual cost. We think we can be near evil and not be touched by it but instead we put ourselves in harm's way. Death is the end result of giving a toehold to evil desire.[52]

Therefore, it is necessary to be wise, circumspect, and realistic about our tenuous place in reality. Most sin comes from overconfidence, from its attractiveness and a failure to acknowledge our limitations.[53] For Eve the fruit looked "good for food and pleasant to the eye."[54] Adam was lured by the appeal of being "like God, knowing (both) good and evil"[55] in what was then a good creation. Cain was tempted to eliminate his rival brother and be the sole survivor before God.[56] The alcoholic is tempted to escape from the hardship of life. For the accountant the temptation may be a short-term profit from distorted figures on the balance sheet, and for a sales person the immediate benefit from deception about the quality of a product.

Hardship, panic from threats to our existence, and longing for power to control life all lead our flesh naturally toward activity contrary to God's Spirit.[57] These are forms of accusation against God's supposed failure to provide what we want; however, the Bible clearly declares God's innocence[58] concerning the sin of Adam and Eve and its results in our daily experience. Instead, it is Satan who is on continual watch to see whom he can recruit for his own earlier rebellion against God.[59]

---

52. Jas 1:14–15.
53. 2 Tim 2:22; 1 Cor 10:12.
54. Gen 3:6.
55. Gen 3:4–5.
56. Gen 4:9.
57. Gal 5:16–21.
58. See *The Innocence of God* (Paternoster, 2007), by Udo Middelmann.
59. 1 Pet 5:8.

All these temptations must be resisted with the common sense we so often lack. We can learn such common sense when we understand with our minds and hearts what God tells us in his word, those letters from afar, about life here in the real world. Temptations are not so much religiously wrong as they are fundamentally stupid and unworkable. They result from wrong ideas, and for that reason we have looked all along at the correct ideas in the Bible.

Chapter 15

A Distinct Ethical Edge

THROUGHOUT THIS BOOK I have suggested that we should recognize and treasure how very different we are from everything around us, even from sentient animals. We are unique in our mental ability to reason and imagine, which enables us to speak, love, argue, reflect, choose, and create, as well as to make factual and moral distinctions. We deliberately use language to speak and label our world, as well as to tell a joke, deceive, or pretend.

Animals function according to an inner program and patterns that we can reasonably refer to as natural laws, what something does by its very nature. In contrast, we are poorly equipped to depend on the material and biological parts of our nature to get those things done which lie outside our limited instinctual patterns; we need ideas and concepts to act. We must choose to love and work, how to dress and what to eat, and to pursue what is right and just. Instincts do not help with these activities. Such daily needs do not take care of themselves, they do not just happen: we need to choose them.

The meaning of the original Greek word *concept* is idea or mental picture. Such ideas come from the workings of our inventive and imaginative mind, from doubt and inquisitiveness rooted in our *inability not to question* the reality and finality of anything. People always want to figure things out. Children ask "why"; adults touch, poke, cut open, and look inside or under the surface to find out what they do not yet know. People imagine alternatives and pose the unanswerable question, "what if."

Ideas also come from other people who can teach us. When they know more than we do because of age, experience, and inquisitiveness similar to our own, they can teach us what they know. Since we are made in the image of God we also get ideas from him. He had ideas before he created this complex reality we inhabit, which he communicates by the efficient and precise instrument of his Holy Spirit's use of human hands, minds, and vocabulary in the Bible.[1]

Our life takes place within the setting of the world around us, our particular time and place. We have active minds that can remember the past, analyze it, and learn from both its good and bad sides, mental activity which then requires us to be selective about what we do in our present moment and the direction we give our lives through the choices open to us.

This realm of choice, governed by ideas which shape and motivate us in a particular behavior, we call responsibility: the ability to respond, explain, and justify to ourselves, our children, neighbors, history, and God, what we do or avoid doing, commit or omit, create or destroy.

When we make mental distinctions between right and wrong our judgments are accurate and truthful in the measure by which they match up with the real world. God expects us to be truthful and accountable so that we can do greater justice to what is actually good and right. The Bible provides additional information from outside ourselves that teaches and confirms in our minds what we lack from our few instincts. A rational, impersonal, natural world has built-in laws but we are designed to make use of gathered knowledge and additional instruction for our choices within an orderly existence.

This pursuit involves some central components that make up a realistic biblical ethic. They intertwine with the working of God's creation and facilitate our life before him and other people.

Foremost, honesty in all areas is central in a world of clearly defined specificity. Things are what they were designed to be in their characteristic structures. People, in distinction, must *choose* to advance and to practice rigorous standards of honesty, since our choices are surprises or disappointments and not part of the world's existing structure. All language depends on the choice for honesty, whether in contracts, conversation, product presentations, measurements, or definitions of meaning.[2]

Let me give some illustrations to shed light on actions that show lack of honesty because they are deceptive, creating an impression without substance, blurring the difference between what truly is and what only appears to be. Dishonesty makes use of the foolishness or ignorance of a person. It uses a lie, a pretense, a cover-up, as a lick of paint attempts to

---

1. 1 Pet 1:19–21.
2. It would be valuable here to review the earlier discussion of honesty in chapter 11.

cover up an underlying fault. It is dishonest to bend the law for personal favors, as for instance through bribery and other forms of under-the-table deals. Judges at court must be free from personal and political influences so that their official rulings are based on the same law for everyone, not on existing friendships or the expectation of receiving personal favors, gifts, or some other advantage.

Honesty requires that movies and software not be pirated and that producers not be cheated out of their wages. It is theft, another form of dishonesty, when things are appropriated without recompense. Theft can be the work of individuals, companies, or governments. Overbilling for work, underperforming in assignments, false statements of content, inflationary policies, wasting company time, and late payment of bills and employee wages[3] are but a few ways that theft occurs in daily life. It not only includes taking what belongs to another person, but also diluting the value of savings, or misusing tax money that should be spent on improvements, security, and services for everyone.

The wise person responds to facts and evidence with honesty. We must value and choose an honest response because we acknowledge that there is real truth above our personal opinions and preferences. We conform to the shape of reality to avoid danger and death; likewise, we should obey the facts of relationships, acknowledging the rule and responsibility of those from whose work and greater experience we benefit. Employees should be subject to their bosses and do what is expected, answering back only to prevent bad decisions by offering suggestions for better ways to accomplish tasks.

Peter refers to obedience, as Paul also does in Romans, in relation to being citizens of a state, whose authority is from God "to punish those who do wrong and to commend those who do right."[4] The text specifically limits the authority of the state and makes king, governor, and parliament accountable to God who will judge them, for they are only second in command.[5] Their authority is limited to punishing evil and providing the good under the same master and law for everyone.[6] We must submit to lawful government to strengthen its effort to do good, so that "the ignorant talk of foolish men" is silenced. As servants of God we

---

3. Lev 19:13.
4. 1 Pet 2:13–17.
5. Eph 6:5–8.
6. Eph 6:9.

are mandated to do good, be respectful in our comments and critiques, support what is good, and oppose evil.

Obedience involves giving honor to everyone as our neighbors, and to the good rule of those in positions of authority. This does not, however, in and of itself require agreement or support for all policies, contracts, and products, nor acceptance of inhuman and unsafe work conditions, or low wages set by the market alone. When participation in an immoral activity is demanded, moral objection out of a desire for improvement is not disobedience, but rather an immediate, forceful statement in the quest for justice, for *adjustment*. It was therefore a sinful error of judgment when German military officers, under their oath of service to Hitler, extended their obedience to the state to include active participation in the slaughter of millions of Jews.

We can not expect to abstain from difficult choices until clear moral circumstances prevail. They do not exist in this fallen and imperfect world. Peter points to the need for realism, delayed reactions, and a willingness to make do with far less than perfect situations in any area of life. The alternatives are often worse, and wisdom requires us to accept that little else may be possible.[7] For that reason he counsels that we should be subject to employers with respect, not only to the good and gentle ones but also to those who are far less than perfect. We then follow in Christ's footsteps by enduring unjust suffering, "doing the will of God from the heart."

Francis Schaeffer frequently admonished people with the reminder that, if you want perfection or nothing, you will always have nothing. This is the honest reality of human life in any area: work, relationships, communities, and public policy are all imperfect in a fallen world. And to that our response is not resignation, calling what is imperfect good enough, but work for improvements in the days and years ahead.

There is then no room for deception or pretense. The honest person does not rely on appearance over substance, on fantasy or flattery. Like all biblical ethics, honesty is rooted in the defined shape of the created world. There are many scriptural references to this emphasis on truth in words, actions, and relationships, including commerce and production, so that all parts of reality match up to a single simple truth: we live in a rational universe where our choices have real consequences no one can run away from.

---

7. 1 Pet. 3:14–21.

Honesty requires that we agree on words spoken, promises given, and common definitions, measures, and timelines. Without honesty, employers and employees cannot work together, marriages will not hold, and contracts will not carry a binding obligation. But when disruptive tendencies in relationships are reduced, when there is no falsehood and deceit, human interaction can blossom, trust becomes possible, and one can get on with the business of life. Otherwise every event is unrelated, isolated, and haphazard and human interactions are random and unreliable.

Jesus reminds us that we should always speak the truth, not only when we are in court and swear to tell the truth. Our "yes" should always express the true meaning the word carries, rather than merely creating an impression or pretending to be the truth.[8]

People function better and are more respected when they reject what the Bible calls ungodliness, behavior, and thinking inconsistent with God's character of light, truth, and love. Ungodliness diminishes our human calling and submits us to uncontrolled appetites and natural passions that rob us of the privilege of making selective moral decisions. Human beings can and should be self-controlled, upright, and wise by leading lives that honor themselves, their neighbors, and the God whose image they should exhibit.

When asked whether taxes should be paid to Caesar, Jesus answers that since the coins bear Caesar's likeness they should be used to pay Caesar for his services.[9] Similarly, since we bear God's likeness we should honor him in all we do. We are made distinct from all else; this, not a life filled with religious patterns and irrational behavior, is what the Bible understands by a godly life.[10]

The challenge in this difficult and often unfair world is to do what we know is right and sensible, to not let go of a critically discerning mind, to see beyond the present situation and persevere even after failures. An employer who sees his investment in an employee as a long-term commitment does not easily abandon him or her but encourages persistence and gradual improvement. We do that already with children from awareness that their development and increasing skills are not automatic, but acquired gradually over time. Like them, we all need encouragement

---

8. Matt 5:37; Acts 5:11; Zach 8:16–17.
9. Matt 22:21.
10. Titus 2:9–14.

along the way to pursue moral and human goals and not be distracted by only slow progress.

The Bible urges us to work toward conflict resolution, both by seeking peace and freedom from the natural chain of push and shove among people, and by mastering challenges. Nature is an endless cause and effect reality but people can create something better when we swallow our pride, make do with less, and walk the extra mile out of our way.[11] Scripture tells us that making peace is critical to our moral health.[12] We forgive in response to the forgiveness we receive from God when we ask to be forgiven. It is not gratuitous, but costly for God and his Son.[13]

Rather than let a situation continue on an endless downhill slide or in a chain of payback and revenge, we can put an end to it and create a new beginning, even if at our own expense.

For God it was worth everything to redeem the damaged situation between himself and his creation. What is it worth to us? Should we not see that we reflect God's character more through reconciliation than through insistence on personal rights, religious acts, and sacrifice?[14]

Revenge is cyclical and prevents a new beginning. It obligates us to what we think of as personal honor, yet responds to one evil with another. It makes us react mechanically and frustrates our calling to freely create a better situation. Jesus teaches that rather than automatically responding in kind when my enemy slaps me in the face, I am free in my sovereignty to think up a surprising response that disarms his evil intentions.[15]

We must embrace anything good that might diminish the harm people do to each other. Life is already harsh enough. Let us not add to it and make it worse through endless insistence on revenge, having the last word, or imposing our power!

This outlook should start with sexual relations, the most central and intimate human bond, where we are so vulnerable and can do permanent damage to each other. Sexual fidelity is the most immediate, personal form of exhibiting and living out love honestly. Whoever cheats here in thought or action is likely to also cheat in lesser matters of work, service, and business, which are not so closely tied to his person and all of life.

---

11. Matt 5:41.
12. Heb 12:14–15.
13. Eph 4:31–32.
14. Matt 5:32–33.
15. Matt 5:39.

Sexuality is a treasure that makes union between a man and a woman desirable and brings the closeness of comfort, trust, and creativity into a unique relationship. Adam could not have this by closeness to God or in proximity to animals. Adam's need for a companion on an equal level could only be satisfied by Eve, another human being who was the same yet different, and attractive to his own sexuality. In their union they could create another generation.

Children are conceived and born from the sexual union of a male and a female who yet remain separate persons forever. Sexuality is then not mere biology but part of a chosen commitment to love, honor, and trust the other person in a marriage involving deliberate separation from all other natural intimate and sexual possibilities. It is a commitment, independent of time and place, to one other person to create a unique life together, greater than either partner could accomplish alone.

The most visible as well as the most secret part of a life together, sexual love in marriage requires a lifetime of ongoing practical moral choices based on prior commitment that recognizes the unique personal arrangements only husband and wife can create and maintain. A couple bind themselves to unshakable promises that span time, are grounded in thought with promises intended to be kept, and make each other worthy of trust.

Without such commitment, all relationships are temporary, subject to a seesaw of emotions and attractions, troubled by hardships, and threatened by better offers. No human relationship can take root and bear rich fruit when either partner can walk away, when intimacy (or company secrets) is not specifically protected by specific commitments.

In any place, whether at work among colleagues, in neighborhoods with other people, or in church communities, in any human proximity within dependent and admiring relationships can lead to sexual temptation. The possibility of greater happiness in a different situation is always attractive in an imperfect world, but should be recognized as something that comes with a high price. Infidelity destroys the previous life, yet can never create the space for a really new life. The "old me" can never become a "new me"; rather than disappearing, it becomes an integral and failed part of what is always believed to be, but never truly is, a new venture.

Only with commitments based on love of self and the other person can trust be built and counted on in any relationship, from marriage to parenting to work. Trust is created and earned over time, not as a right but as a reward when we prove worthy by faithfulness to the demands placed on us.

Our commitments need to be confirmed and fleshed out in word and action. It is a light thing to make a promise but far more arduous to mean and keep it.[16] Consistency and courage are required to think through an assignment, promise, or obligation and then carry it out. Commitment comes with consequences and diminishes previous freedom: it means one cannot simply walk away.

It is important to work on being trustworthy, for otherwise our commitments will fail in our temptation toward personal benefit and gain when other opportunities arise.[17] The Bible furnishes an historic example of failed trust in the fascinating and tragic account of Saul's failure to carry out the assignment he had received when he was made king over Israel. The people had insisted on having a king like all the other nations around them.[18] But when God finally consented and raised up Saul as king, he betrayed God's trust and did not punish the Amalekites, a tribe that had repeatedly opposed the Israelite migration into the Promised Land.[19] Instead Saul tried to profit from the spoils of war, and like so many other rulers, managers, and business owners, lost the trust placed in him by God and his people.

It is important to work on one's trustworthiness, as the nature of commitments in general and the consideration of factors like personal benefit and gain has removed trust as a concern. Commitments between spouses in marriage or between owner and employee in business easily fall prey to temporary personal considerations, priorities, and opportunities. When the single guiding principle in a person's life is whatever is possible, morality can easily be trampled underfoot to fall by the wayside. Commitment is rarely seen as a decision with consequences that diminish the freedom one had to make that commitment. It needs to be confirmed and fleshed out in word and action.

For many people today, the commitment to a partner in marriage is a choice for the moment, "as long as love lasts" or "until I find a better offer." What began as Friedrich Hegel's philosophy of dialectic history and then was developed in Marx's teaching is now widely accepted. In

---

16. Eccl 5:4ff.
17. Prov 20:6.
18. 1 Sam 15.
19. Exod 17:8; Num 14:25, 43, 45; Deut 25:17; Judg 3:13; 1 Sam 15.

A Distinct Ethical Edge

this view every moment of history has its own justification and there is no lasting meaning to words, promises, and value choices. Instead of long term commitments based on enduring distinctions between right and wrong, decisions are now largely made on the spur of the moment in response to changing situations and variable personal taste.

The antithesis of "either—or" has been replaced by the embrace of "both—and." Critical analysis has been abandoned in favor of an encompassing synthesis. What once had a stable definition is now understood to be continuously emerging. The formerly unthinkable becomes first thinkable and then also doable, as if all of life were on a slide, passing through and abolishing former opposites so that what was once considered life can be cruelly violated by death.

In such thinking every moment of history has its own necessity and is thus emancipated from any larger moral obligations that do not carry weight over time. There is no reason to justify a change of plans or keep a promise. "Whatever is, is right" describes a cosmic evolutionary motion in which all events are essentially necessary simply because they happen. Rather than analyzing what is good and right, logical and beneficial, synthesis opens the door to all manner of contradictions.

Some Hegelians are fatalists in the belief that all events and situations simply follow a timeline like ducks lined up in water. Everyone can sit back and watch what is happening without judging or being obliged to question it. Absent any moral distinctions, every situation is a new opportunity without restraint, shame, or contradiction. Everything becomes doable because it has become thinkable. Since all history is merely evolving, any contrary actions are undertaken free of guilt. Thus one's immediate life is independent of and more real than any prior commitments to spouses, workers, students, or children.

Other Hegelians embrace the same view of a forceful process of history to deliberately provoke conflicts in order to advance the universal dialectic process faster. They are the revolutionary activists without moral restraint who overthrow whatever framework stands in the way of the progress they envisage.

With that mentality, we owe no one allegiance and we are all free to act on the spur of the moment with our feelings justifying our behavior. When history (the earth, nature, providence or traditions) is the ultimate explanation or reference point there is no room for moral distinctions. If everything must be accepted, man loses his place and obligation to stage a *coup d'état* against evil.

A trustworthy, reliable, and secure community will only exist where moral values derived from the Bible shape and direct relationships in all areas of life. Biblical moral values bring our thinking back into line with the nature of reality first, and then also with the character of the uniquely true and living God.

Paul addresses these issues in his advice that our schema, or pattern, of life and thought should be distinctly relational, respecting people and their common needs. He writes of the philosophical basis for this in 1 Thessalonians,[20] and Romans 12 provides basic principles for healthy personal relationships. In other passages Paul also discusses aspects of such relationships. When we set out to love our neighbor as ourselves, we should be sincere.[21] Love is a choice to build bridges to another person, just as our choice to love God has substance only when it is a choice to keep his commandments. The awareness of our own need to be loved lets us imagine that our neighbor also requires the same. The uniquely human ability to put ourselves mentally into another person's place should be a great help in loving our neighbor. Love is not anxious, but honors the other more than myself.[22] Our calling is to serve our neighbor with all our abilities, including our wealth of personal intelligent insight (what we know), our compassionate emotions (what we feel with sensitivity), and our material resources,[23] including hospitality[24] (bread to eat and water to drink). We must also be patient when life does not proceed smoothly or brings only affliction.[25] We share a life with others, including time, attention, emotions, and frustration, and we are to be deliberately sensitive to what they experience of hardship, disappointment, illness, and worry,[26] and relieve them as much as possible.

This practice of commitment to relationships creates a culture of engagement and incentive, work and effort, and accurate accounting and precise craftsmanship, freeing us to be human and make moral judgments about what is otherwise merely natural. Love is a choice, the hard

---

20. Especially chapter 1:9–10 and 4:1–13.
21. 1 Cor 13:4–7.
22. Phil 2:3.
23. Rom 12:13; Eph 4:28.
24. Heb 13:2.
25. Ps 30:5; 1 Peter 5:6.
26. Rom 12:14–18.

work of an intelligent mind in recognizing and solving real problems, real suffering, and real injustice.

This biblical outlook of appreciation for each human being encourages improvement and change and gives true significance to individual people along the timeline of history, where each day is unique, not the template for the next in an endless cycle of ugly continuity. Without this perspective any community, business, or individual lacks the motivation and insight for real creativity and will consequently only repeat what has always been acceptable, just good enough, and commonly done. Our greatest resource, the human mind, will be stifled and its human potential wasted with no profit for anyone.

Improvements begin with ideas developed in the mind; we first desire and imagine, then plan and decide. We receive instructions for those choices from life, from our conscience, and from the Bible. We should especially nurture ideas transmitted from the Bible that can be the basis of our enterprise, hope, and deep confidence: we are loved personally, we live in a purposeful and fundamentally orderly world, and our wise and committed investment in people and the things they can accomplish can bring about real rewards.

Appendix 1

God and Man at Work

Foundations of Social Capital Development

This appendix serves to present a more detailed outline of the basic Biblical foundation for the text. In any project, whether in construction, in business or even a marriage, a foundation is laid first in the mind, in one's considerations based on desires, possibilities and hopes. There is always a beginning. The groundwork is then laid, decisions are made and then built on.

"In the beginning" of a person's life and the start of conscious questioning is always a human being, whose different desires, hopes and plans will contribute and influence what follows. The Bible starts with a human perspective by presenting a Being with a specific personality, existing already before any 'beginning', i.e. eternally. Neither energy nor matter is eternal, but personality is! They thought, loved and created people to bear God's image, to love them and to be bound to them contractually, in covenants.

This unique Biblical perspective in its development throughout the text helps to explain how people in some societies developed greater skills and more creative, entrepreneurial attitudes in their social, economic and political life. They became more independent of their external circumstances like geography or weather. Their world of ideas provided a sensible, effective and realistic framework, within which individual people and neighbors in society found encouragement and approval for their efforts to improve life. They saw the need to review their situations, to discern what is good and saw reasons to reject what is harmful and destructive and, in the larger scheme of things, foolish and wrong.

The appendix furnishes a network of ideas presented in the form of propositions about the real world. They address everyone in response to the need and desire to know the kind of world we live in. Life itself, human existence, throws the questions at each person, whose mind wonders, questions and seeks a context for every experience. No one should despair, clamp up or blindly follow a group's common ideology bound up in traditions or religions. Instead everyone should look for those propositions that knit together a coherent view of origins, existence and purpose and thereby lay the foundations for a productive, humane and rewarding life for all. Many communities, cultures and traditions still continue to impoverish, humiliate and exploit people, particularly women and the uneducated.

Change towards a richer human existence has borne fruit largely among people who have examined and acknowledge the validity and truth of the propositions laid out in this curriculum.

The appendix follows the much longer text of the book itself, which gradually constructed from many details the framework of insights which helped people since a long past to step out of passivity into creative activity and to abandon the impression of only being forgotten victims of circumstances in a meaningless history. The book addresses the causes for widespread passivity, fear, a sense of boredom, and insignificance. It describes daily work as a creative effort not only for survival, but as a way to show that persons matter, because each individual act of learning, thinking and doing confirms a person's singular humanity 'in the image of God'. Through work and words, through love and artistic effort, through many forms of creative intervention people place signposts of human presence into an otherwise impersonal world. Nature is not the home that produced people. Instead, it does require personal moral, creative and enterprising intervention to make nature, including human nature, more fruitful and less threatening.

Both book and appendix seek to teach individuals to bear responsibility for their own lives in work, business, society and relationships. Natural curiosity and increasing inquisitiveness helps each person inevitably construct a view of the world from observation of life, from instruction by others and his or her own reflection. It becomes their intellectual house, with one or more rooms furnished by divers experiences. Under its roof they learn to be able to somewhat hold their own through trials, learning from failure and growing with accomplishments.

From early childhood on and through the time of being in school and becoming working adults all of us seek to know how and why everything around us functions. We match components of the external world to ideas, hopes and fears. People are unable not to wonder and seek, at least initially, to understand life in all its facets in order for it not to constantly overwhelm by its frequently contradictory and harmful components. A truthful, coherent and honest understanding of "whence, what, whither" existence shall indicate a direction to grow in and to then become good and knowledgeable parents to the children of the next generations.

Nobody sets out or arrives alone. Each person is part of a larger community. That can be their emotional and geographical home and give some security through habits and a common language. However, it can also constrain and tie persons to old habits of thought and practice without encouraging review, new discoveries and change for the benefit of many. Societies can both embrace individuals with new ideas and reject individuals for threatening an established status quo, a collective consensus, a life shaped largely by authorities which impose their will, power and traditions.

An education should make each person go further. It should lead each person, on his or her own initiative out (Lat.: *e-ducare*) of a cycle of repetitions in a collective, using freely examined convictions and improved insight. Raising questions and seeking answers that make sense and help construct a coherent view of the world has a liberating effect. It is the first step of freedom from reciting old sayings and following uncertain and often questionable values. Strings and attachments that prevent new ideas also impede better work habits and needed insights about the material world to make life safer. The mind needs fitting explanations, and the body greater protection against disease and death from whatever source. A liberated heart and mind goes beyond what others have already done, always in search of improvements to benefit everyone.

Such advance and improvements are by no means automatic. In many societies all approaches to life have been largely finalized in shared religious traditions and social obligations. Repetitive patterns stand in the way of personal efforts, new skills and a rich moral imagination, which are needed to overcome the hardships and limitations in nature and communities, which burden each person in every generation.

Jewish and Christian teaching in the Bible has a different emphasis. Where it was taught in the form of propositions as an explanation of life in the real world, it stands out as a constant reminder to real persons of two driving ideas that promote effort, progress and the benefits of real rewards. The first idea is that of a rational universe, the creation of a loving and benevolent, thinking and resourceful God, who made persons in his image. That is good news in a world where chaos and contradictions, fear and loneliness, an impersonal and uncaring nature, and finally death seem to be the dominant features. God's real existence creates an intellectual and emotional home for human beings. All other propositions declare them to be misfits, alone, and always threatened..

The second idea proposes that all experience of a painful normality in daily life is in fact the result of a tragic, weighty and very consequential destructive choice in real history by the first people. Their pursuit of wanting to 'be like God' destroyed until now what before they had experienced as a good world. The now normal world is in fact no longer an evidence of the character of God, but damaged, fragmented, shattered and full of contradictions, profound unfairness and under "the dust of death". This proposition supports our necessary awareness of real distinctions in reality rather than imposing, as religions and ideologies do, the quest for harmony as somehow more important. It explains the pain and frustration familiar to everyone, but also mandates to find ways to resist evil and death in any of its many ugly faces. It gives people a vantage point above the daily grind to interfere rather than to submit to the flow of history or the collective opinions of people. Water always runs downhill and fire always consumes, but people need to distinguish between true and false, real and imaginary, actual and possible, mine and yours, man and beast, and finally also between God and idols.

These two ideas call people to be creative agents for good and for resistance to evil; to stand up and work against decline, ignorance, injustice and any other form of sin, which is at the base a disregard for God and his creation, for things and people alike. The God of the Bible does not show his intentions in what happens all the time in history, but in laws and instructions to clarify and harness what is just and unjust, good and evil. The teaching and life of Jesus Christ, who is God in real time and place, exemplifies his opposition to all manner of wrong. In both forms of God's WORD a clear foundation is laid for a future judgment of all people do now, first through their children's and later generations, and after that also in history by God.

The proposition that things in all of life are not what they were originally meant to be gives liberty and every encouragement to each person to recognize evil, imperfection and injustice and then to seek ways to correct the flaws. It removes passivity, fear and hopelessness by renewing the mandates to each person to live and act as people made in the image of the creator. People are not the children of nature or the community of men, but of God.

Whenever these two central ideas were taught and understood in their significance, they formed the background for improvements in all areas of life. They removed any form of passivity or fatalism, spoke against any finality in situations and opened doors for enterprise by the use of the mind, of hands and of natural resources.

Most religions and secular political systems without the influence of Biblical teaching lead to resignation, to accepting what happens by the will of gods, elders, or a political class. Where the Bible was taught and understood to explain reality more accurately, especially in relation to the place of human beings in the course of time and in different places, it awakened creativity, moral discernment and economic opportunity such a significant role that all other authorities, religious, political and tribal, were challenged. People became agents of God to get things done in history and for the benefit of many.

For, according to the Bible, God's work is not finished and wrong and evil and death must not be tolerated. The God of the Bible invested himself to clear things up, as well as to promise and deliver real healing through the work of the Blessed One, who from God would make all things whole again. In Jesus we are loved and accepted by God, and his resurrection is the powerful evidence of the conquest of death and the healing of nations.

Live, work and craftsmanship; love, justice and peace in the community; healing of bodies and minds and relationships: each and together they are professional opportunities for each person. Skill is required in each of them, and that skill has to start with skillful discernment about the nature of reality: of God, Creation and the Human Person.

Appendix 2

In the Beginning

The Basic Content of the Biblical View of Life, Work and Society

The scene of a play, the stage setting, is very often described at the beginning. In that way the location, the time, the persons and their place or role in the play are introduced to give the framework for the interaction about to happen.

The Bible provides the same structure. It starts at the beginning with an introduction to all of existence; we are the present participants and actors.

I. The answer to the "question of origins"

(How everything got to be here) sets the tone for everything that follows: in knowledge, in attitudes, in your view of life for people and all things. Consider what each element in the account proposes to your mind and lays out for it:

1. Genesis 1:1 "In the beginning God created. . ."
   What does this propose?

   A. God exists before 'the beginning': A personal being decides to create! Our world is part of a personal universe.

   What follows from this proposition, what does this imply?

   B. Unified, rational God who explains = orderly creation.
   Single authority, without conflict, competition, rivalry.

C. Creation of everything exists outside of God, vis-à-vis, separate from God, not an extension of God; not everything is God or part of God. There is one eternal God, all else is created.

D. God chose to create: purpose, goal, order to get it done.

E. A sequence to God's work, thought; not all at once, final, terminated. God still works, acts, intervenes 2:5

2. Genesis 1:2-end What of the "Seven Days of Creation?" What does this suggest?

   A. Gradual purposeful elaboration and additions/variations.

   B. Unchanging, original definition: Water is not land, wood is and remains just that: "Each according to their kind". "Fixed laws with heaven and earth" (Jeremiah 33:25); Reliable definitions of things and people as persons.

   C. Changing dynamic, gradual, active: linear history with a goal in mind. Every day is different, new possibilities: invites innovation, review, improvements, exploration of alternatives. Resistance to traditionalism: The past is not always good or sufficient enough.

   D. Land produces living creatures (1:12,24), dynamic interaction

   E. Real effort, delight, variety; "all very good."
   (Genesis 1:4, 18, 21, 25, 31)

3. Genesis 1:3, 6, 9, 14, 20, 24, 26 "And God said. . ."

   A. Specific attention to increasing diversity: God speaks, thinks and actuates designations, terms, concepts, definitions.

   B. No finished product, static power, closed end: distinct beginnings followed by continues interaction (chemistry and physics, fertilization) passing through developmental stages, evolution. 2:4–6.

   C. Continuous creation through Man, using specificity of materials, defined particular things/animals to form new composites, structures, varieties. 1:28–30.

   D. Good creation: "Pleasing to the eye, good for food" 2:9; 1st Timothy 4:4.

4. Genesis 1:26 Creation of Man, male and female.

    A. God formed man and woman, not natural: Dust + breath of life; 2:7, 22.

    B. In "the image of God", a person: mind, emotions 1:26.

    C. Equality of Male and Female 2:21, 22.

    D. Man and woman mandated to shape and populate earth 1:28–30; 2:15.

    E. People are wanted, loved, attended to 2:15–17.

5. Genesis 1:28ff Work/cultural mandates.

    A. Human existence intended for earth, not heaven 2:15–17, 20–25.

    B. Mandates to subdue, to have dominion: work with intellectual and manual tools.

    C. Unfinished creation, changes intended, open plan for God and Man: freedom within the form of the real world.

    D. True creativity, requiring knowledge to respect form, and freedom to discover extensions into new areas.

    E. Real choices offered: to name, shape, invent, discover.

    F. No repetition, no imposed dictate: grow, improve, vary! Admiration for God's work and human accomplishments.

6. Genesis 2:15ff Life together under God and with one another.

    A. Defined freedom, love, obedience, experiences.

    B. Choices for life, truthful, lies lead to death.
    Significance within form creates inescapable consequences. Example: marriage, work and idleness, choose life or death Deuteronomy 30:11–20.

    C. Reject knowledge and experience of possible evil 2:16f; Matthew 4:1–11; James 1:2–8;

    D. Life under God, but unity, help with/from spouse/family Genesis 2:20—25;

7. The lure/temptation of any 'ideal', even though really impossible experience.

In the Beginning

   A. (Not a question of knowledge or ignorance) i.e. "You shall be like God."

   B. Fall brings knowledge, i.e. experience, of Evil/ death.

   C. Loss of what was there before; now a fractured existence. Genesis 3:8–24.

8. Genesis 3:8–13 (1st element of fracture: Moral wrong).

   A. Moral effect/break with past: hide from God: Gen 3:7.

   B. Legal death: Sin, guilt and shame. Gen 3:9—11.

   C. Mutual accusations, suspicion, broken relations: Genesis 3:12–14, 16b.

9. Genesis 3:14—20 (2nd element of fracture: Physical damage).

   A. Life in a damaged world: Physical difficulties.
   Increase in conceptions, pain in birth. Gen 3:16
   Ground difficult, thorns, weeds, labor sweaty
   Genesis 3:17–19.

   B. Physical death: "dust to dust" Gen 3:19.

   C. Greater effort to defy death, quarrel, despair: The Bible's instruction, plea and encouragement in history!

10. Genesis 3:15 and 20 Hope for and in the Future.

    A. God picks up work on 8th day, extra effort for situation.
    Genesis 3:9, 15

    B. Promise of victory over evil and death.
    Genesis 3:19, 1st Thessalonians 4:13ff; Isaiah 61ff

    C. Future generations to break death's reign.
    Genesis 3:20

11. Genesis 4:1–14 Cain and Abel (Religion or Truth).

    A. Believe God's instruction, don't invent a religion!
    Genesis 4:2–4; Hebrews 11:4

    B. Tendency of sin, we are damaged human race.
    Gen 4:6,7; 6:5; Romans 5:12

    C. One human race, brothers' keepers.
    Gen 4:9; Lev 24:22; Number 9:14; Acts 17:26

In the Beginning

    D. God's continued presence, concern, help. Genesis 4:14, 15; 2nd Chronicles 6:14fff

12. Genesis 4:15 ff Life continues.

    A. Cain lives, works, builds, has family. Genesis 4:15–26.

       Arts and crafts, manual and aesthetic work. Genesis 4:19–22. Activity, enterprise: crafts, builders, shepherds, traders, bankers, fishermen, farmers, artisans.

    B. People call on the name of God 4:26; Isaiah 45:14ff.

II. Life skills in an imperfect/damaged world

Recall the following:

- God is not in nature/creation:
- God's mind and character expressed in a text:(language: meanings, sequence, grammar of words); written and living word (Jesus, the exact image of God the Father) to the inquisitive and discerning mind.
- Prophets ("mouth/speaking for God")
    - sent to correct false views/behavior and argue for truth.
    - Jesus is Son of God.
    - Holy Spirit to inform, correct, comfort with hope.
- Everything now imperfect, under the dust, in shadow of death.
    - Man's thought & body; all nature, politics, history.
    - Tendency to conflicts: hate, dishonesty, injustice; death.
    - Life is a choice! Jesus as true 'Water', 'bread', 'light' from God.

1. Genesis 4:26b (and 6:5)—chapter 11

    - Frequency and nature *of human failure in responsibility.*
        - *Adam's personal failure: accusing Eve.*
        - *Cains moral failure: killing his brother from envy.*
        - *Noah's social failure: no regard for neighbor's life.*

In the Beginning

- *Tower of Babel: Human ontological failure: wanting to replace God.*

A. Significance of each individual's action/choices.

B. Knowledge of God not steady, complete, not everywhere, needs frequent study, reflection, exploration, renewal.

C. Depends on integrity of people: needs discernment, integrity; not repetition or mere collective agreement (Job 1:22).

D. Some people are righteous because they think and live rightly (Genesis 6:9; Job 2:3,9) What is "right"? Obedience or truthfulness? True to reality of God, reason and reality.

E. Individual choices have social consequences over generations (Good and bad kings, priests, spouses, natural situations require action. No passivity.)

F. Image of God unchanged, not lost in human being through bad choices, sin (9:6; Leviticus 24:16).

G. Rich world of ideas, imagination, art in language, objects and reflection. Human life contains poetry, inventions, personality.

H. Power of false, unrealistic, ideological views as well. What then? Ideology as effort to create imagined "perfection" (i.e. a collective, obedience, submission, order, form), possible when efforts stop, all changes forbidden, individuality is suppressed.

2. Tower of Babel (Genesis 11)
   - Freedom from God required creation of a divine human purpose:
     - "A name for ourselves, lest we be scattered" Gen 11:4.
     - Collective, common social goals are no protection against error.
     - Genesis 11:1,4.
   - no sufficient substitute for God, the false belief in invented explanations of reality. 11:4.
   - community insufficient to give moral focus, destroys awareness of necessary clarity; Words and values diverged into multiple value systems. 4:7, 8.

In the Beginning

- With insufficient grounding in true universal, no particular construction/society can last: either dictator or social chaos.

3. Abraham and God's contracted promise (Covenant).
   A. Called God's friend. 2nd Chronicles 20:7; James 2:23.
   B. "God in heaven" contrasted with Chaldean nature deities, part of creation e.g. 'Sin" (Moon),'Shamash' (Sun),'Ishtar'(star). Jeremiah 10.
   C. Intellectual vs. sensual comprehension. Ephesians 4:17–19; Genesis 12:1 "God had said."
   D. Believed God to tell the truth. Understands words with informed sense, reasonable mind, discerning thoughts. Genesis 12:2–3; Isaiah 45:19.
   E. Necessary reflection to discern truth from falsehood. Faith and action working together.
   (James 2:22; Hebrews 11:17, Jeremiah 10:6–14).
   F. Rejects visual, sensual, feeling idols as criteria for truth: Genesis 12:4–9; Jeremiah 10:14ff.
   G. Individual discernment and moral choice for integrity e.g. Genesis 13; 15; 18.

4. Nature focused (pagan) search for appeasement ("lie low") vs. God's Covenant promises ("stand up and go") Isaiah 45:20–23.

- Think through and discuss these opposites: Describe the effects of each element in both sides in and on cultures. Give examples:
  - make peace with the /// Receive peace from God
  - ground/nature
  - Human sacrifice for gods /// God's sacrifice for people
  - Silent Idols /// God speaks, acts, gives text
  - Cruel nature is natural /// Nature needs human labor, change, inventions
  - Blind obedience to rulers /// Argue with God for truth (Job, Jeremiah)
  - With rulers, false teachers (Elijah)

- Authoritarian /// Authority
- Nature/history remains same /// God and Man alter, improve, oppose, repair, interfere

"Do not conform to the pattern of this world, but be transformed by the renewing of your mind" (Romans 12:2); "Don't live by the standards of this world" (2nd Corinthians 10:2); Ephesians 4:23.

5. Promise of future restoration:

    A. Promised 'Blessing' to Abraham's descendents as nation and as believing community. Genesis 12:3; 32:22ff; 49:9f; Deuteronomy 6:10ff; Isaiah 45:4.

    B. Tomorrow a truly new day, not a repetition of yesterday Biblical accounts relate to events in history with choices and effects.

    C. Directional, linear history with efforts to improve, invest, repent: Consequences, change, new; lasting results for all.

    D. "Salvation" of soul *and* body (both fractures) in history: every step/effort/work helps and anticipates full recovery. Redemption from sin/guilt; from physical death in new life. 1st Thessalonians 1:9,10; 4:13ff; 1st Corinthians 15:1-ff. Embrace of life, work and reason/observation, science, facts (vs. faith, ideology, irrational assumptions, fear of the unknown) Js 1:22-25.
    Hopeful and active, vs. insignificant and passive approach to life, work, thought. Each individual causes enduring effects/waves. Isaiah 45:18.

III. Social teaching, effects on society

1. Life is currently fundamentally unfair, but has not always been this way:

    - God is not behind or approves all events; He grieves. Genesis 6:6; Exodus 32:14; 1st Samuel 15:11,35; Jeremiah 1:16; Job 34:18-22

- Unfair history now, since true significance of all burdens many others later with unmerited, unjust results: Job, Luke 13:1–4; fair history only in future Ezekiel 18: "Soul who sins will die."
- Reason, love and justice are not natural, but personal efforts to limit effects of fall/sin/error. Genesis 18:19; 2nd Samuel 8:15; Ps 17; Micah 6:8.
- "Love the neighbor as oneself", because he is foremost a human being as well. 'Love' foundational to personal relationships: bridge builder, investing more than returned: Rom. 12:9ff; protection of his life spheres: Ex 20:16; Leviticus 19:13–18; Deut 5:21; 19:14; Prov. 3:29; 25:9; Matthew 19:19; Mark 12:31; James 2:8, etc.
- Laws correct flawed interpretation of real world; they do not create a new reality or power structure. Not rule for assembly, but description of how reality is constructed: Exodus 20; Deut 5; 6.
- Admonitions through prophets to change social direction.
- Seek justice, create health, encourage faint, teach ignorant, fight corruption of mind, law, power, body, nature: Jeremiah 1:16; 2:5f; Ezekiel 3:16ff; Hosea 4:1ff; Joel 1:2–5; Amos 5:6ff; Obadiah 10; Micah 2:1ff; 7:2ff; Nahum 1:3ff; Zephaniah 1:5ff; Malachi 2:17ff; 3:8ff.
- One Law for everyone: Protection *of* and access *to* Law affirms both dignity of each person and restrains each person's desire for power. No favoritism to anyone.

2. General Cultural Consequences

- High view, worth of each person as a person in his distinct nature; not from title, religion, common acknowledgement or late accomplishments: Kings, simple people, prophets, fishermen, children named.
- Equality, rights, privileges, obligations under same law for all persons, in including fair measures, courts, property rights. 1st King's 21:2–19.
- Society, rulers, products, services in constant review, unending improvements, corrections; variety through innovation.

In the Beginning

- Take responsibility: Punctuality, hygiene, faithfulness, accountability, acceptance of instruction, and participation in team. An example to others: 1st Timothy 4:12.
- Responsibility and compassion for others: colleagues, trainees, teachers, neighbors, later generations, environment.
- Pursue further training, general education, and improvements in skills.
- Understand life in full context: answers to Whence? Why? Whither?

5. Moral/ Ethical considerations for individuals/society:
   - Foundation for a moral and ethical life and for society.
   - Note that each of Ten Commands are given in a form that prevents neglect, wrong, evil, harm and destruction. Avoidance of what breaks up life and leads to death, so that we can live, worship and work.
   - The 'form' is given to prevent death, the 'freedom' is ours to explore!
   - Given as reminder to clarify distinction from Egyptian thought and practice: Distinction of truth from religion; a new way of life and work.
   - Given in preparation for Promised Land, after wilderness wandering, doubts, objections: Deuteronomy 5.
   - To be read by Kings: Deut 17:18 -20 "So that he may revere God and follow carefully all the words of this law. and not consider himself better than his brother and turn from the law to the right or to the left."
   - No one is above the law: 1st Kings 2:1–4; 2nd Chronicles 17:7–9; 2nd Kings 22:8.
   - To be read every seven years afterwards: Deut 31:10–13.
   - Read by Ezra after Babylonian Captivity; Ezra 8:1 - 18 .

- Nobility of manual and intellectual work: mandates to change nature to culture; use resources to create, form, discover, distribute what is needed for life.

3. Particular Cultural Consequences

    - Emphasis on unique persons, of any age, of either gender, any skill or state of health. Family links precede all others.

    - Youth sometimes wiser: David 1st Samuel 16:7ff; 17:14; Zechariah 2:3, Timothy (1st Tim 4:12); Amos 1:1.

    - Human person differs from every thing (!) in creation with mind (heart) as source of concepts and speech, imagination, ethics, work.

    - Image of God evidenced in thought, emotions, choices, plans, hopes, belief, ability to love, invent, think abstractly of options.

    - Education of a person to become independent and remain compassionate; private property for benefit of many.

    - Skills developed for dominion/ to comprehend creation and make use of it for all.

    - Think philosophically: raise questions, doubt, argue: Only recognized problems get a solution.

    - Develop aesthetic sense, as a further language to speak, show, embellish, alert and comfort anyone unawares.

    - Become generous, servants of others: Walk 'extra mile.'

    - Moral reasoning before political measures: "What is right, just, fair, rather than what works."

    - Concern about the 'means' precede interests in 'ends.'

4. Personal Cultural Development

    - Respect, value, love yourself: history flows from your character choices.

    - Honesty Integrity, commitment, discipline, focus.

    - Respect, master and enjoy, love work, understand how one ca shape the world around you. Imagine improvements, vari tions, develop safety, practice skills.

In the Beginning

IV. The Why and What of the Ten Commandments

1. Why no other God besides the one who brought Israel our of Egypt? No other God (outside the Bible) explains both: *form* of world, order, logic, reason, structure and *"personhood"* of people. People are no accident, mistake, or wrong development as choice-makers, inventors, creators in their freedom to expand, correct reality.
   Why is it foolish to believe another god?

2. Make no idol, image to worship. Deut 5:8–10
   God is eternal, not a projection of human desire or need. Idols are made by and subject to humans in their presence; God is creator of people, who are always in his presence.
   What central desire of yours could become an idol? Work, pleasure, money?

3. Not misuse the name of Lord your God. Deut 5:11
   Truth stands by itself, not only when referenced to God. Using "god-words" does not add credibility, power, merit, power, respect.
   How does an oath not make a false statement true?

4. Observe the Sabbath as holy. Deut 5:12–15
   To remember that God created persons distinctly. They are not produced by nature. Only people make choices, live seven days by work on six days. Everything else exists the same every day naturally. People should rest on Sabbath from burdens of life in fallen world.
   How can you show that you as a person are not a piece of the natural world?

5. Honor Father and Mother Deuteronomy 5:16
   Because without them you would not exist either. Does not mean always 'like', 'approve of' or 'obey'.
   What do you do to show that you honor parents?

6. You shall not murder Deuteronomy 5:17
   God intended eternal life, not death. Loving neighbor, everyone, like oneself. Influence moral character of others, not remove them from life.

In the Beginning

All life, not only beautiful, powerful, healthy, born!
How can you value and protect a life?

7. You shall not commit adultery Deut 5:18
Marriage is a private intimacy, years of trust and commitment, building a life together. Everyone has only one father and one mother biologically. That private bond is smashed, killed, destroyed, when a third person is drawn into it. A divorce does not create a new situation, as neither person can abandon their past choices: they to carry them along.
What protects the intimacy, privacy of marriage?

8. You shall not steal; Deut 5:19
Everything belongs to someone, created by someone. God owns the whole world he created. People own what they or someone worked for. Stealing pretends that ownership is unrelated to work, effort, investment of ideas, money and time.
Inflation, pretended quality, lack of punctuality are samples of theft! What kind of theft do you know? Make a list of obvious and hidden, subtle forms of theft.

9. Don't bear (or give) false testimony Deut 5:20
Importance of character and truthfulness. Truth in fact, in words and trade is indispensable to all human relationships. Without truth, there is no trust or safety, no honesty or agreement. Lies deceive, destroy and create suspicion.
Think how truth is essential to a rational way of life.

10. You shall not covet what is your neighbor's: Deut 5:21
Contentment and charity reject envy, jealousy, anger, which destroy integrity and prevent steps of improvement from example of others. Resentment over what others have, seeks to destroy their advantage, so that in the end no one has it anymore. Everyone is poorer for it. Inequality is not always injustice, but also serves as attraction to do better.
Distinguish between envy (wrong) and desire to acquire similar skills and things within reach.

V. Intellectual and cultural development on Bible's orientation

- All Bible's laws expound love for God and love for neighbor.
- Law given to prevent ignorance, confusion, evil, conflict, neglect.
- Obedience, submission, faithfulness are consequence of the relief felt from description/revelation/affirmation of such a God.
- Love is primary factor, motivation, pleasure, enjoyment of God, human life, creation.
- Knowledge and love diminish hardship of life in fallen world.
- Love expressed in concern, compassion, generosity, risk taking.
- Intellectual peace with God frees energy to focus on task of life Food and shelter.
- Division of trusted labor, advantage of specialization.
- Education, health and work skills, employment, business.
- The rule of law: both protection under law and equal access to law.
- Judiciary under law to fight evil, corruption, unjust powers.
- Social services and provision to diminish unfair painful reality.
- Benefits of aesthetics as enrichment of circumstances, art in service of a richer intellectual, cultural, emotional life.

www.ingramcontent.com/pod-product-compliance
Lightning Source LLC
Chambersburg PA
CBHW060607230426
43670CB00011B/2008